AF227700

An Illustrated Tour

Color Your Way Through Laconia's History

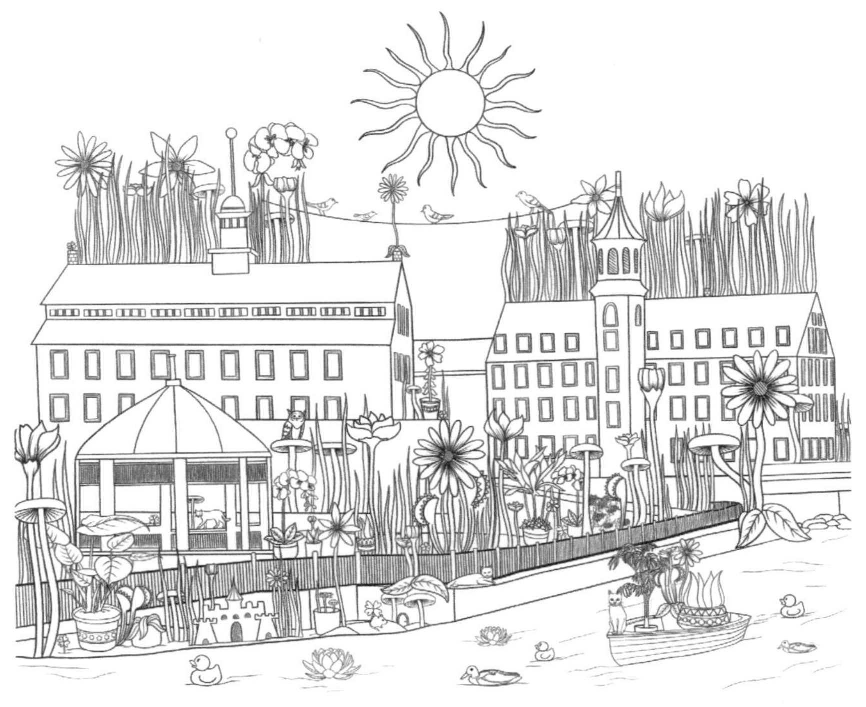

COURTNEY PARSONS   **HEIDI SMITH**

An Illustrated Tour
Color Your Way Through Laconia's History
by
Courtney Parsons & Heidi Smith

Library of Congress Control Number: 2021922803

Paperback ISBN: 978-1-7354250-9-2

Book Cover Design: Courtney Parsons

Historical Research: Heidi Smith

Book Design and Layout: Pamela Marin-Kingsley

Book Editor: Jane Stucker

Give a Salute! provides publishing services to the author(s) specifications and approval. The author retains all responsibilities and rights to the content of this book.

Contact for More Information:

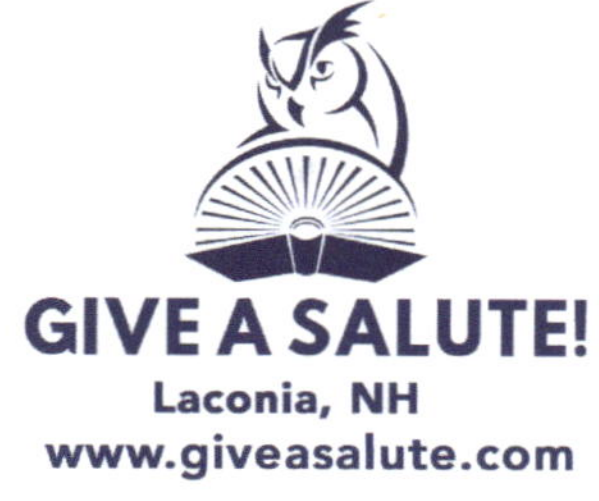

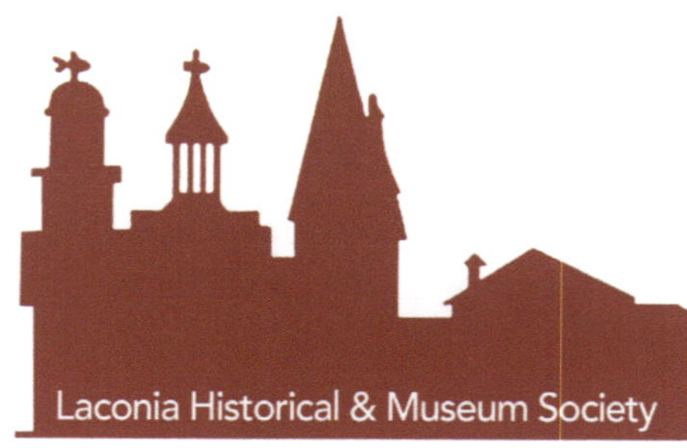

www.laconiahistory.com/

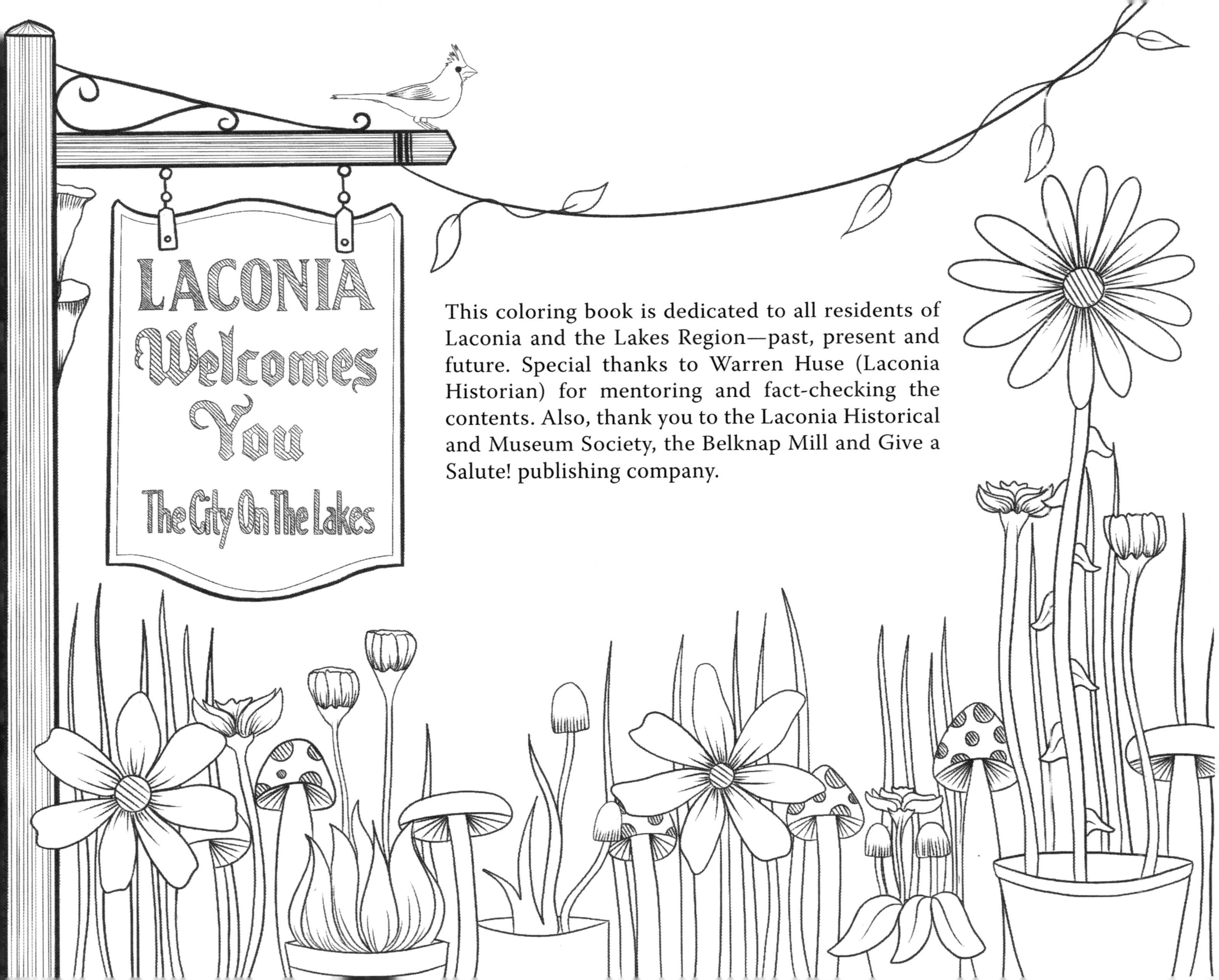

This coloring book is dedicated to all residents of Laconia and the Lakes Region—past, present and future. Special thanks to Warren Huse (Laconia Historian) for mentoring and fact-checking the contents. Also, thank you to the Laconia Historical and Museum Society, the Belknap Mill and Give a Salute! publishing company.

LACONIA–CITY ON THE LAKES

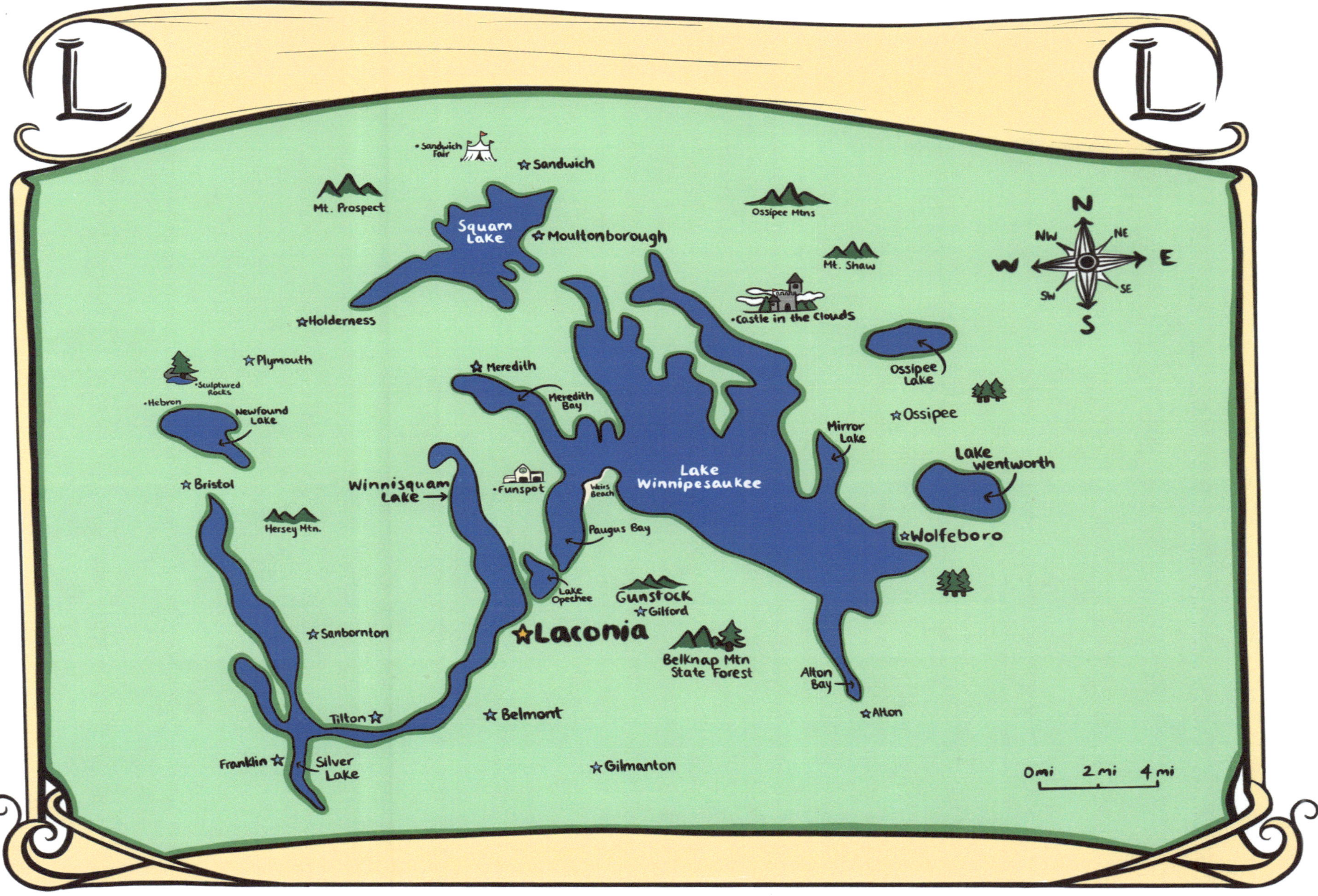

Laconia, New Hampshire, is the seat of Belknap County. Located near the geographic center of the state, the "City on the Lakes" (Winnipesaukee, Paugus, Opechee, and Winnisquam) was incorporated as a town in 1855 and as a city in 1893. When the first settlement occurred here in the 1760s, part of the community was in Meredith and part in Gilmanton (Gilford after 1812). The early hamlet on the Winnipesaukee River, on the site of today's Downtown area, was known as "Meredith Bridge."   From Images of America Laconia by Warren D. Huse

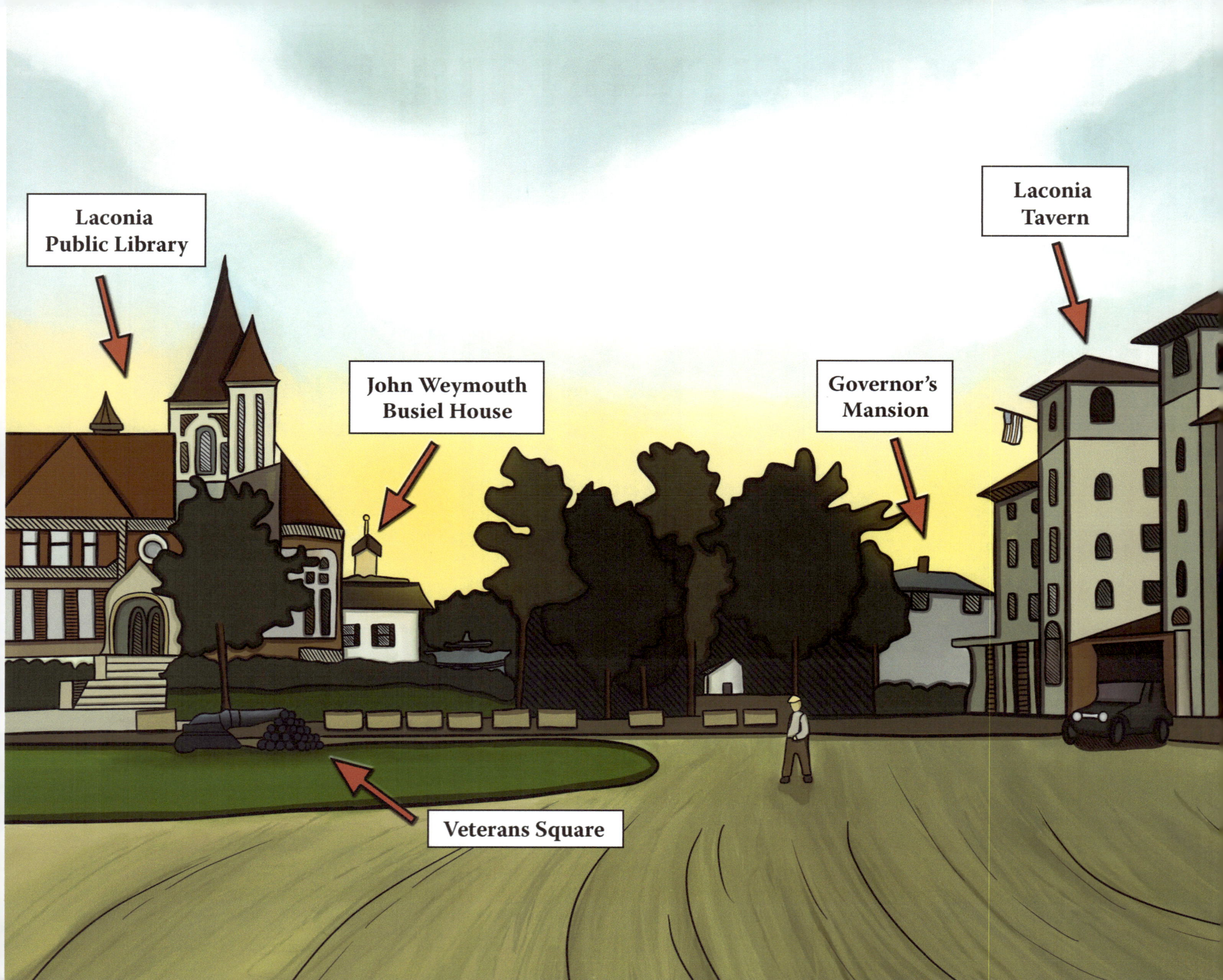

Laconia Public Library
Laconia Tavern
John Weymouth Busiel House
Governor's Mansion
Veterans Square

LACONIA, NH

Main Attractions

Every town and city has its celebrated landmarks, its major buildings, and parks that everybody locally knows about and that tourists to the area are encouraged not to miss. Laconia, NH, is a city like this. Anyone visiting quickly learns where where the public library, historic tavern, Veterans Square, John Weymouth Busiel House, and the Governor's Mansion are. No tour of the city would be complete without seeing or mentioning these historical locations.

In this section, we are giving you a quick tour of these sites which are all located close to one another in downtown Laconia. We have also provided descriptions of these notable places. However, the focus of this coloring book is about the other equally amazing sites that are sometimes forgotten about when exploring the City on the Lakes.

Laconia Public Library

At the 1878 Laconia town meeting, voters raised $1500 to establish a public library. Opened in 1879, the library was first located in a rented room in the Folsom Block. It moved to the Laconia National Bank building and then to the vestry of the Unitarian Church.

Napoleon Bonaparte Gale, a local banker who was known to be generous and kind-hearted, made provisions in his last will and testament for a permanent monument to his memory. A public library was to be built where books, historical treasures and works of art would be kept and shared. Funds were also provided for the creation of a community park.

John C. Moulton, prominent businessman, willed a portion of his land, located on the corner of Church and Main Street, to the city of Laconia. This site was to be used for a public library memorial or other public building. The City later bought the remainder of the property as additional space for the library grounds.

Construction of the future library began in 1901 and was completed in 1903, with the dedication in June of that year.

In 1957, the addition to the library building was completed. It included a children's room, the Martha Prescott Auditorium, and a work space area. In 2005, that addition was removed and a new addition built.

Fun Fact: A reflecting pool was located on the library property. From 1903-1906, an alligator called this pool home in the summer. The alligator wintered at a zoo in Meredith.

John Weymouth Busiel House

Located in the background behind the Laconia Public Library is the Busiel House. This home belonged to John Weymouth Busiel (1815-1872).

Busiel was the eldest of seven sons and one daughter of Moses F. and Relief Busiel. In his youth, he was determined to become a woolen manufacturer. He first worked for his great-uncle, Lewis Flanders, who carded rolls and made flannels and cloths. At nineteen, he went to Amesbury, MA, where he was employed in a woolen mill and learned his trade. He returned to NH and settled in Meredith for ten years. He then relocated to Laconia in 1846 and built the Busiel Mill in 1853.

John married Julia M. Tilton in 1841 and had four children. The eldest was Charles A. Busiel, who went on to be governor of New Hampshire.

Veterans Square

The cannon and cannonballs in the front of the Laconia Public Library are located at Veterans Square.

At the March 1884 town meeting, Laconia voted $2,000 to erect a soldiers' monument. However, it wasn't until 1892 that the park was created in conjunction with construction of the Concord & Montreal Railroad passenger station. The area was then renamed Depot Square, replacing the existing Depot Street which had several buildings on it that were moved elsewhere. On November 7, 1921, Depot Square was changed to Veterans Square by the City Council.

Through the years, several monuments and plaques have been added to the park to honor and memorialize our veterans. An obelisk was erected in late December 1902, to honor the Civil War veterans. In 1903, condemned government cannons, cannonballs, deliberately oversized, were brought in and placed at the park. A reflecting pool, "Keeping the Light On," was unveiled following a "Support the Troops" rally, May 31, 2004.

Fun Fact: In 1944, a Douglas fir, a "living Christmas Tree," was planted during World War II by the Laconia Garden Club, "to bring some joy to the people of Laconia during these dismal war years." A later plaque lists the tree as the "Bob Dearborn Memorial Tree, in Memory of 'Laconia's Santa,' 1932-1996."

Governor's Mansion

The building in the distance on the right is the "Governor's Mansion," or the home of Charles A. Busiel, first mayor of Laconia, 1893-1895, and the governor of New Hampshire, 1895-1897.

Charles was the eldest son of John W. and Julia (Tilton) Busiel. He attended the public schools of Laconia and the old Gilford Academy. After he graduated, he worked at his father's hosiery mill and eventually entered into partnership with two brothers as the J.W. Busiel & Co. hosiery business. In 1864, he married Eunice Elizabeth Preston. They had one daughter, Frances E. Busiel.

He expanded his business interests into railroads, banking and the publishing industry. He was president of the Laconia National and City Savings Banks and the Lake Shore Railroad. He was also a director of the Concord & Montreal Railroad.

Laconia Tavern

Benjamin Piscopo was one of the several local businessmen who was involved in having the Laconia Tavern constructed in 1912-1913. Later on, New Hampshire Gov. Murphy was the owner; still later, it was the Stafford Family; after that, the Laconia Housing Authority.

On June 13, 1913, the Laconia Tavern opened and had 75 guest rooms, most with private baths. It provided hotel rooms for tourist, transients and several famous people, and many local organizations used the dining room and function rooms for meetings. The dining room was said to be "the place" to go for special events and parties. Esther B. Peters, local broadcasting pioneer, at one time even broadcast her radio show "Around Town" from the hotel coffee shop.

Fun Fact: In addition to President Eisenhower's visit in 1955, Richard Nixon, Edward Kennedy, John F. Kennedy, Estes Kefauver and numerous other prominent persons stayed overnight or held functions at the Laconia Tavern. After Prohibition ended, the Laconia Tavern installed a bar frequented by, among others, Grace Metalious, the author of the book Peyton Place.

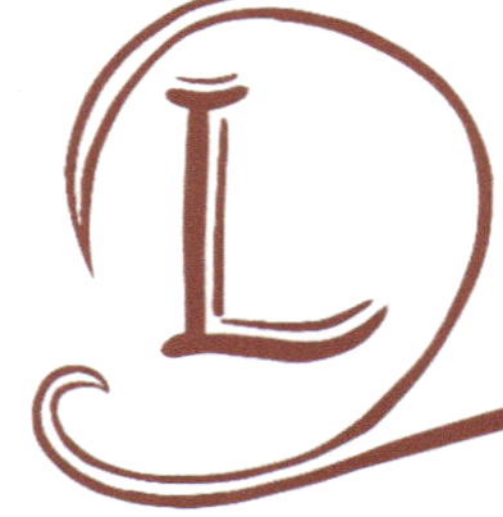
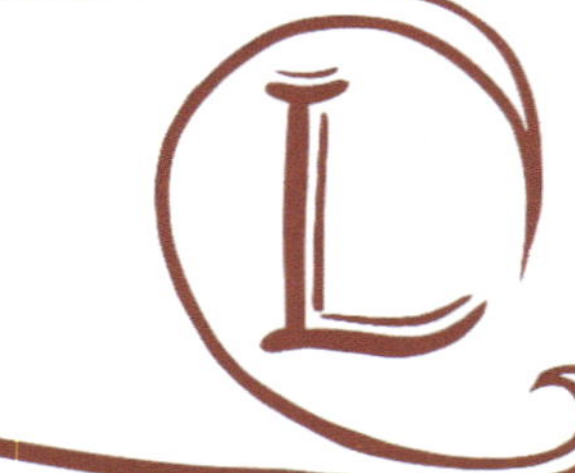

Christmas, Downtown Laconia

This photo captures memories of yesteryear of Bank Square during a holiday season in the 1960s.

The F.W. Woolworth five and dime store, seen in the background, opened for business in early November 1937, and was a holiday shopping favorite.

Santa's workshop was usually located next to the passenger station at Depot Square but was occasionally set up in Bank Square. In both locations, local children would line the streets for a chance to see Santa and ask for that special gift. Like any good Santa, however, he was making a list and checking it twice so he could find out who was naughty or nice.

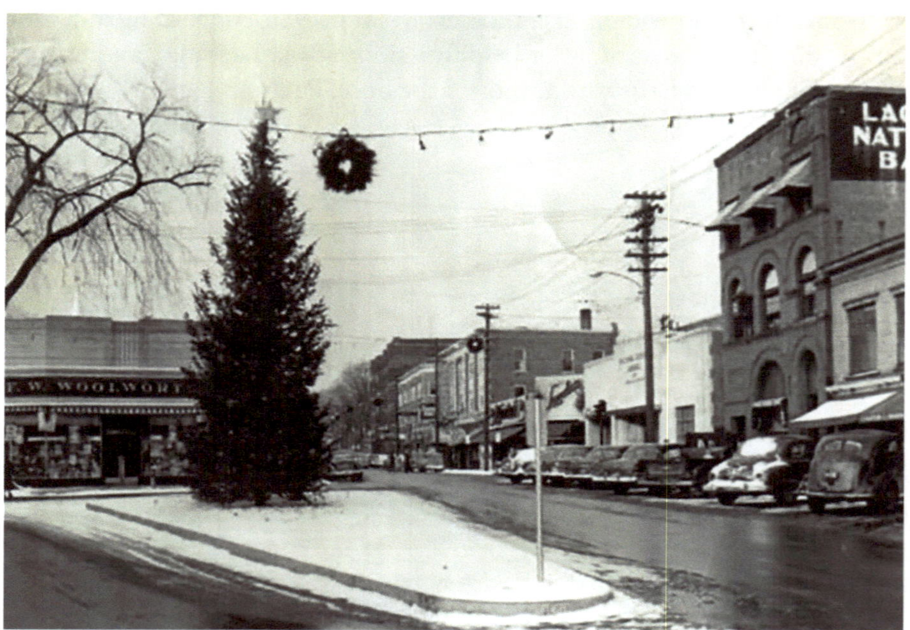

From the Lakes Region History Online Collection

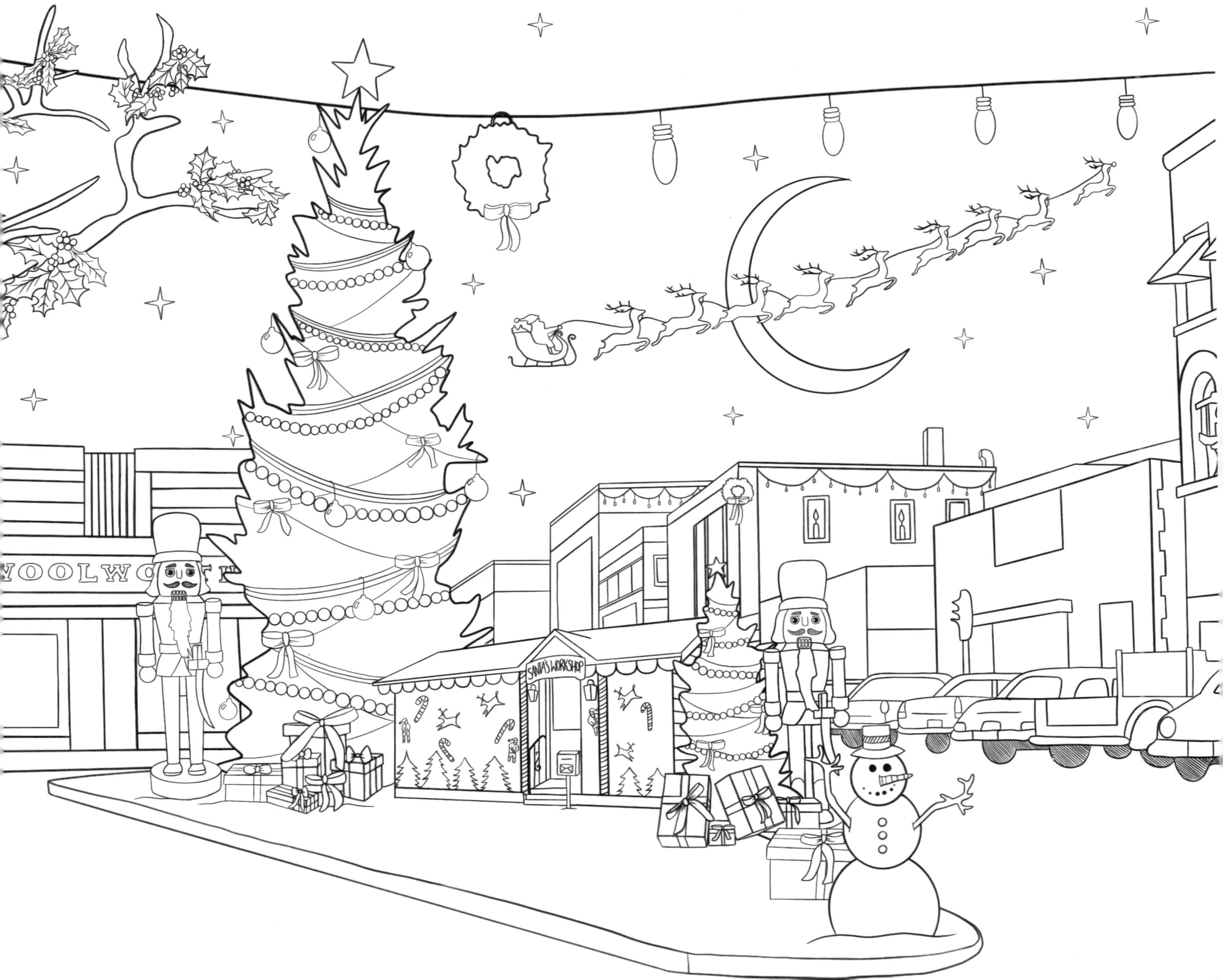

WOOLWORTH
SANTA'S WORKSHOP

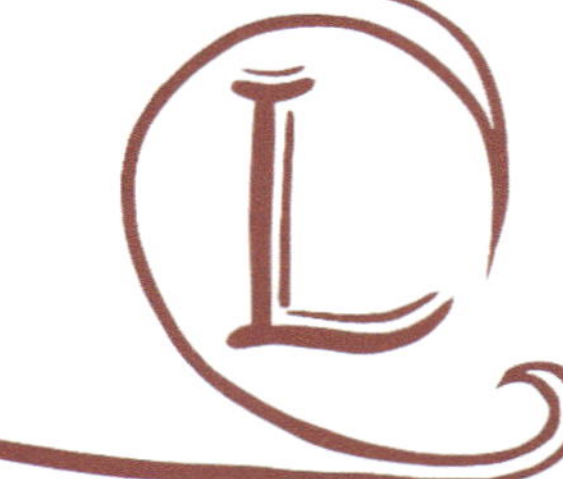

The Colonial Theatre

The Colonial Theatre opened in 1914. Benjamin Piscopo was the original developer of the theatre.

Over the years, the theatre featured vaudeville acts and stage productions and from the first year it also showed motion pictures. The stage was as large as those of the standard playhouses in the big cities, and every seat in the house was positioned to have an uninterrupted view of the stage.

In the early 1980s, the theatre was subdivided into five smaller screening rooms.

In July 2003, the theatre closed after 89 years of operation. However, in 2021, the marquee would once again shine bright and the doors would open again to welcome a new generation of folks to enjoy this newly-restored and renovated venue.

Fun Fact: The Gardens Theatre competed with the Colonial through the '30s, '40s and '50s. They were right across the street from each other. The Gardens mostly showed second-run B movies and children's shows—cartoons, shorts and westerns—on Saturday mornings. The last movie shown at the Gardens was in 1955.

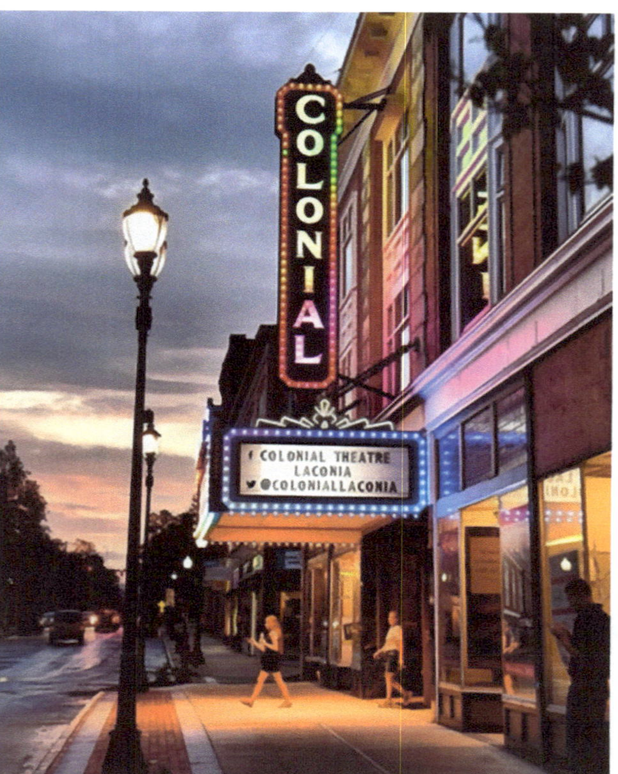

Photograph by Colleen Phaedra

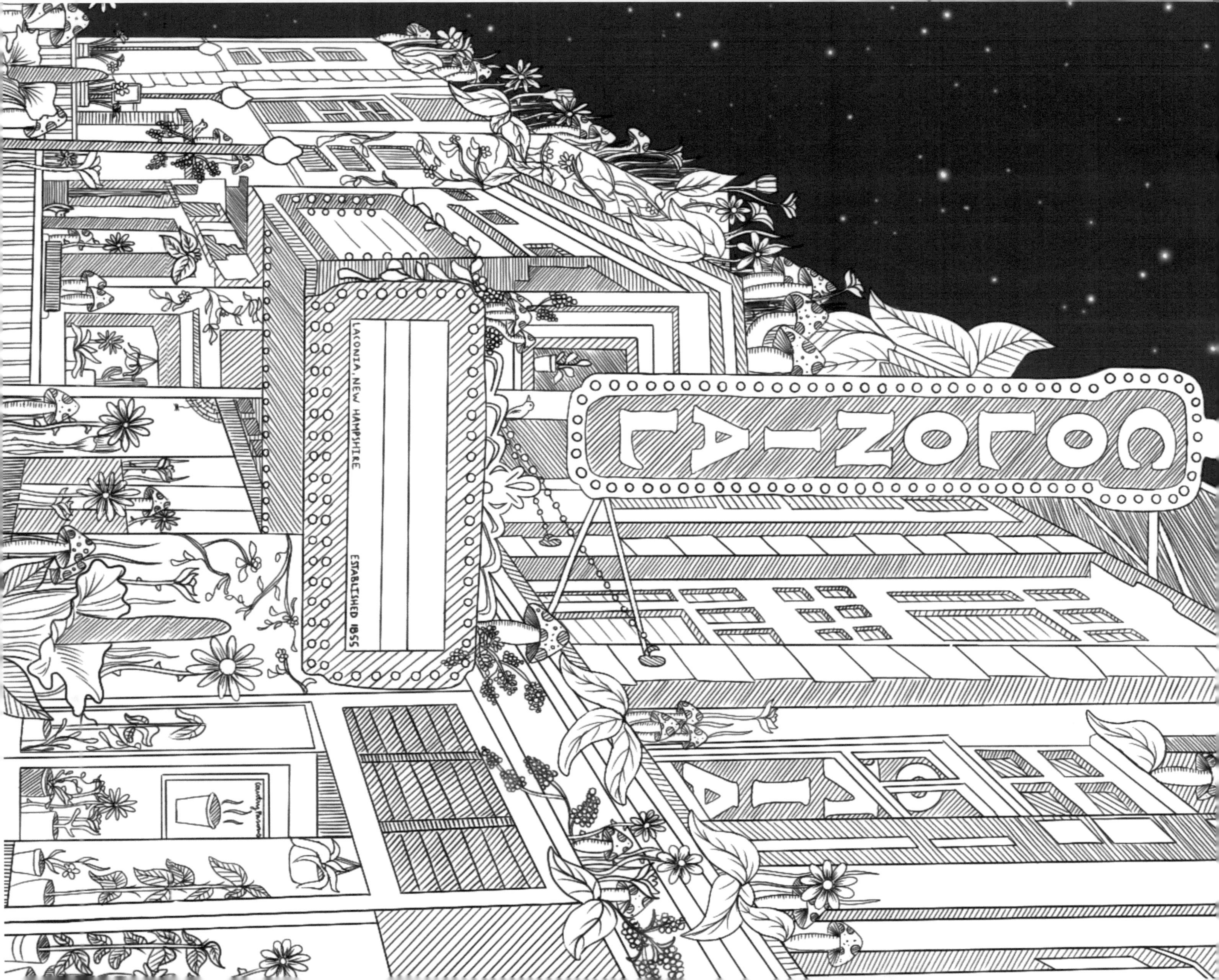

LACONIA, NEW HAMPSHIRE
ESTABLISHED 1855

The Mills

Meredith Cotton and Woolen Co. Mill: This was one of the first mills for the manufacture of cotton goods in the country. The initial meeting of the company was called on July 1, 1811, and the mill was built and in full production by 1813. Shares of stock were issued and sold to the citizens from Gilford and Meredith; land was purchased by Stephen Perley, and a large wooden mill was erected on the site by today's Belknap brick mill.

On February 13, 1823, a fire broke out in this mill and within minutes the wooden structure was engulfed in flames. The mill was lost.

Fun Fact: The first bell that hung at the Meredith Cotton and Woolen Co. Mill was said to be cast by Major George H. Holbrook, a former apprentice to Paul Revere. The bell was destroyed in the fire.

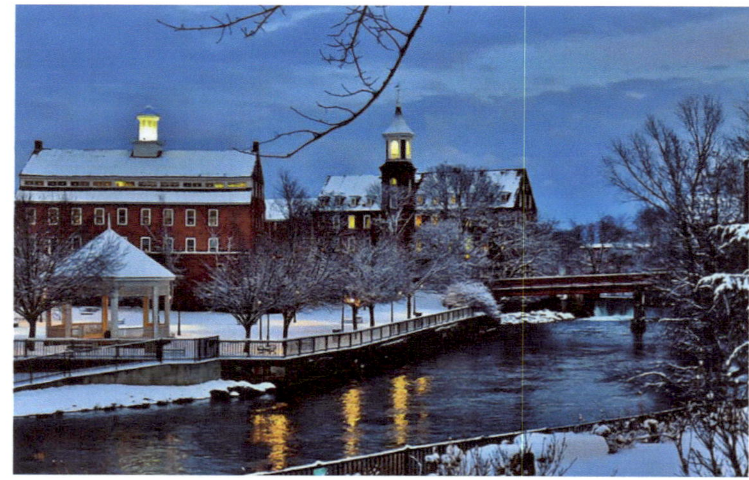

Photograph by Joanna DeCesare

The Belknap Mill: In 1823, a new mill was erected and operational by 1828. This mill was made of brick, and the clay for the bricks came from Eager Island in the Winnipesaukee River, near the Fair Street railroad trestle.

The Belknap Mill is the oldest mill in the United States, essentially unaltered from its original construction. It continued to produce cloth and hosiery until June 1969. After that a successor company, Belknap Industries, moved the operation to a location on Fair Street where they continued to produce socks for a number of years.

The Busiel Mill: Built in 1853 by John W. Busiel from Moultonborough, NH, and doubled in size in 1877-1878, it initially manufactured cloth and later hosiery; subsequently, it was used for the manufacture of clocks, electronic relays and organs.

During the Civil War, the demand for hosiery was so great that the Mill's only business was manufacturing socks for the soldiers.

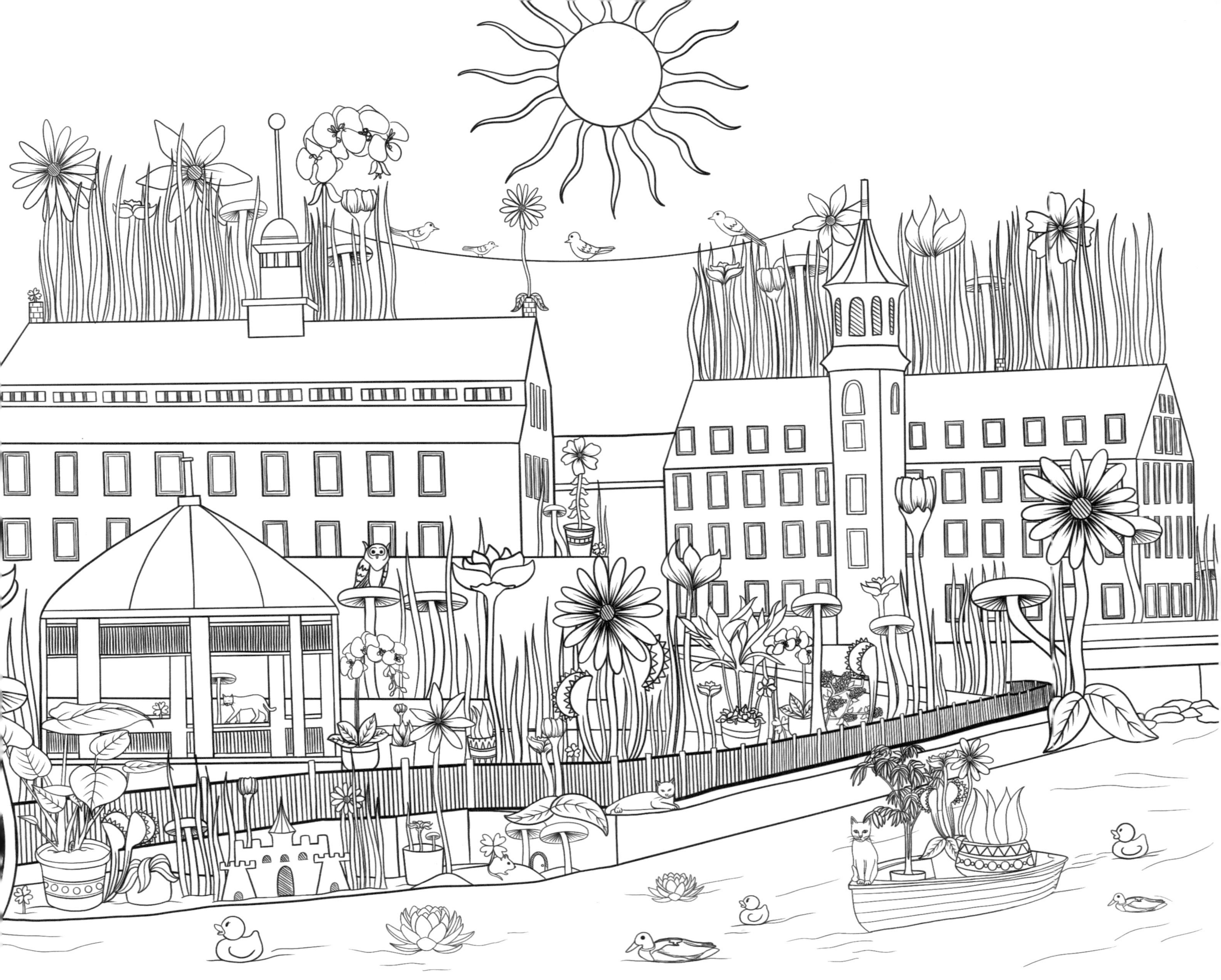

Goss Reading Room

The Goss Reading Room, located at the corner of Elm Street and Franklin Street in Lakeport, was bequeathed in the will of Dr. Ossian Wilbur Goss.

The land where this quaint gable-roofed brick building now stands was once the home of Dr. Goss's father, Dr. Oliver Goss, and Ossian moved into the home after his father died in 1896. This home was destroyed in the great Lakeport fire on May 26, 1903.

After the fire, and before his death in 1903 at the age of 47 and 6 months, Dr. Goss willed that a portion of his estate be used to construct "reading rooms" on the site of his former home "for the use and enjoyment of the general public of Lakeport." The rooms were to be "kept open at all seasonable hours; to be provisioned with all the latest magazines and at least three daily newspapers; to be heated and lighted when necessary; and furnished with suitable furniture." He had intended to re-build his home on this parcel of land, but he passed before his dreams of a new residence were fulfilled.

A trust was established to carry out Dr. Goss's wishes, and on April 8, 1907, the small library that carries his name was finally opened and is still open to the public today.

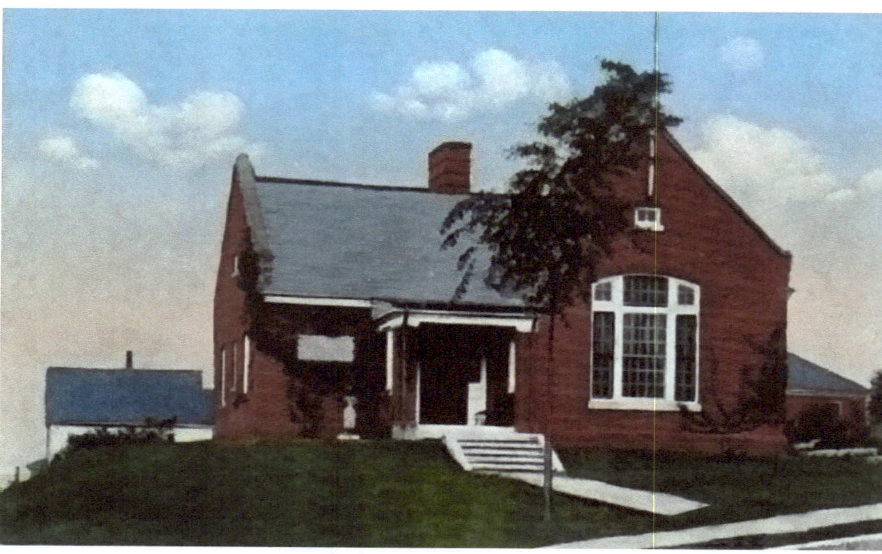

From the Lakes Region History Online Collection

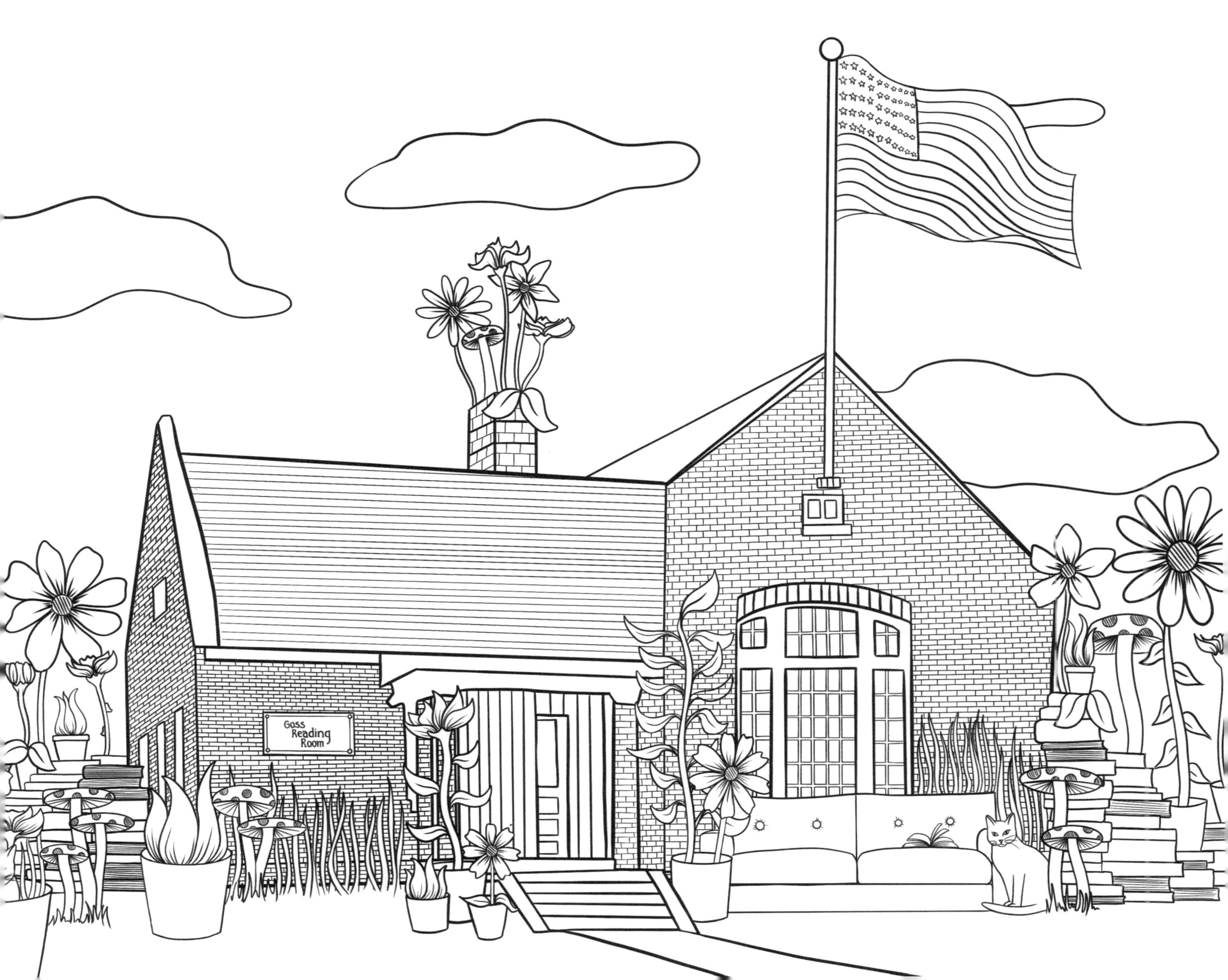
Goss
Reading
Room

Hathaway House

Samel C. Clark, a prominent attorney in Lakeport, (then called Lake Village), built a substantial home in 1871-1872, at 1106 Union Avenue, north of today's Dunkin' Donuts.

Clark was born in Lakeport on January 9, 1832, and died on March 19, 1897. He and his wife Clarissa had three children. Their son, Samuel Clarence, born in 1857, died in infancy. Three years later, Clarissa gave birth to twins: Samuel Clarence, (known as Samuel, Jr.), and Claribel.

In September of 1957, Richard and Constance St. Clair bought the Clark homestead. They turned it into a women's clothing store and gave it the name Hathaway House. After it closed, a number of businesses occupied the mansion, including a restaurant of the same name from 1977-1981.

In mid-March 1982, the barn at the rear of the former Hathaway House opened as Summerfields Spirited Dining. In early April 1985, Fletcher's, a lounge located on the lower level of the restaurant, opened. The barn burned down in a fire, Sept. 19, 1991; the house was demolished, Oct. 28, 2014.

Fun Fact: Local legend has it that Claribel's ghost had stalked the mansion ever since her death in 1953.

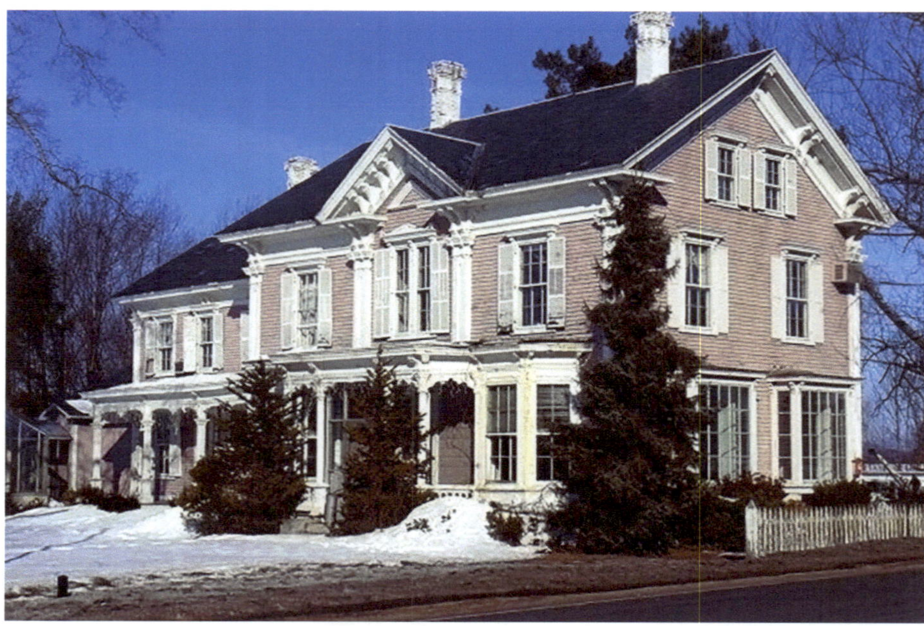

Photograph by Daryl Carlson

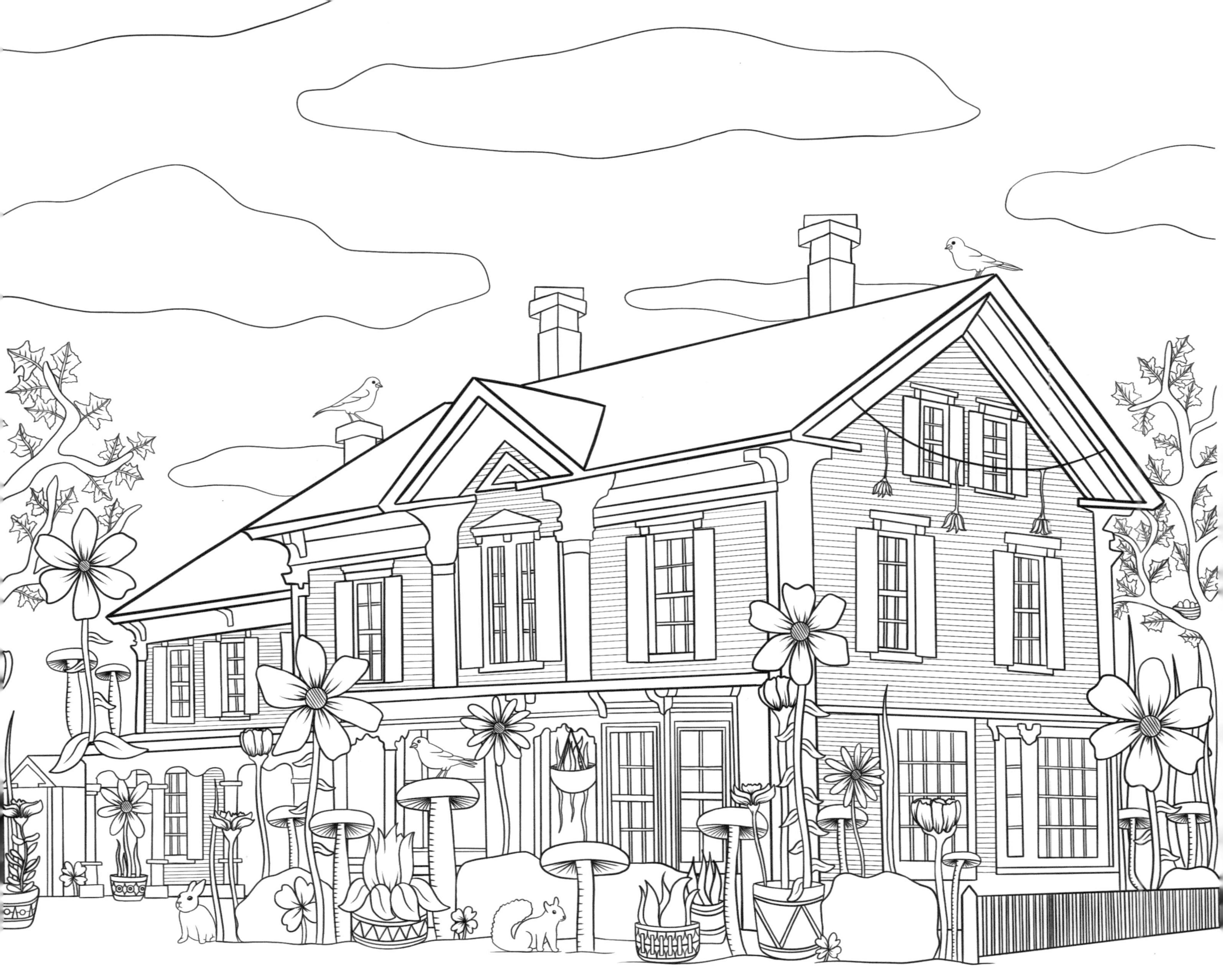

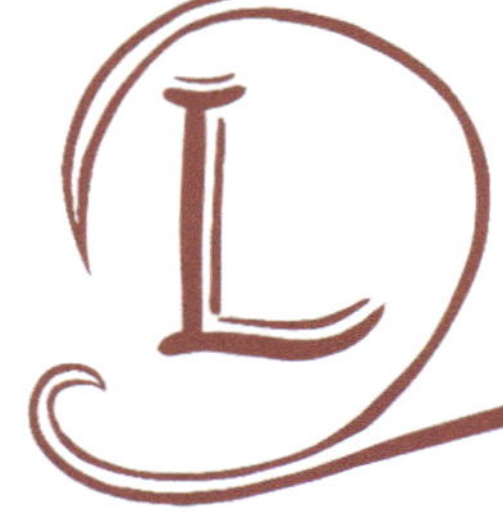

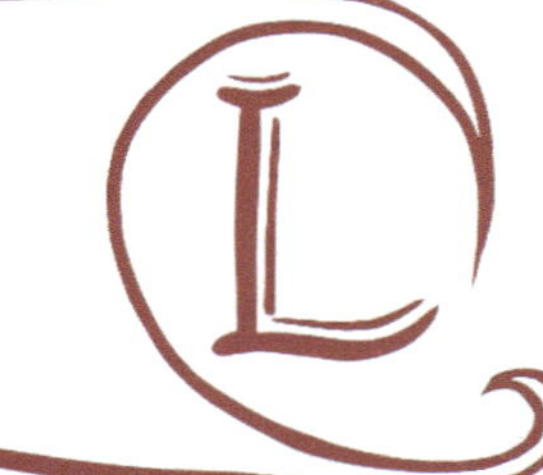

Lakeport Opera House

Lakeport Opera House was built in 1881 by Joseph C. Moore and his son David. It was originally named the Moore's Opera House and seated 250 people. The stage was on the second story of the building. It hosted plays by local groups and traveling companies, concerts, minstrel shows, local social events and vaudeville shows.

Fun Fact: In 2015, the 'Grand Drape' that once graced the stage of the opera house was discovered by Brenda Kean, past executive director of the Laconia Historical and Museum Society.

The Drape is about 20 feet, 6 inches wide and 13 feet, 6 inches high. It was painted by John Gannon of Boston in 1907, and depicts a scene of treeless mountains, a church next to the water, and a castle-like structure in the center. In the foreground, a young woman is carrying an armful of sticks along a winding road.

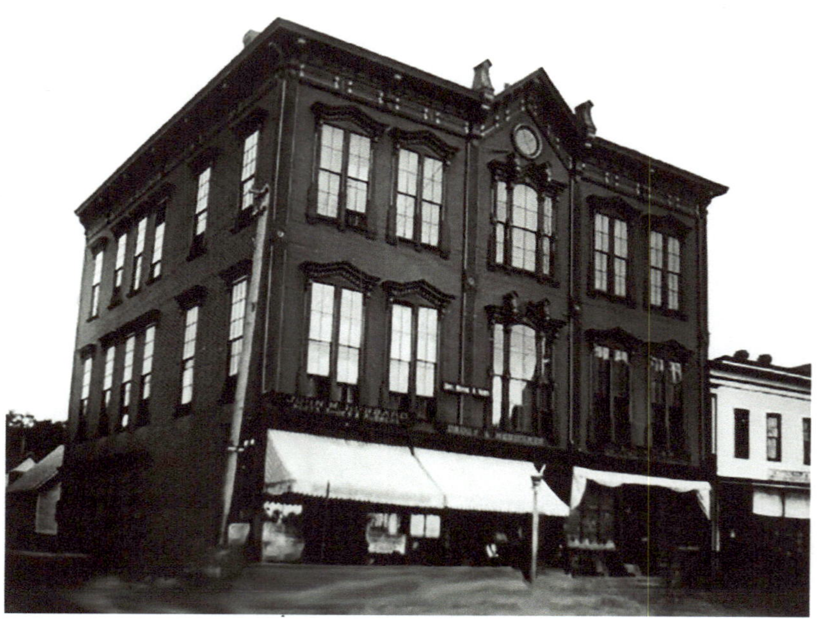

From the Lakes Region History Online Collection

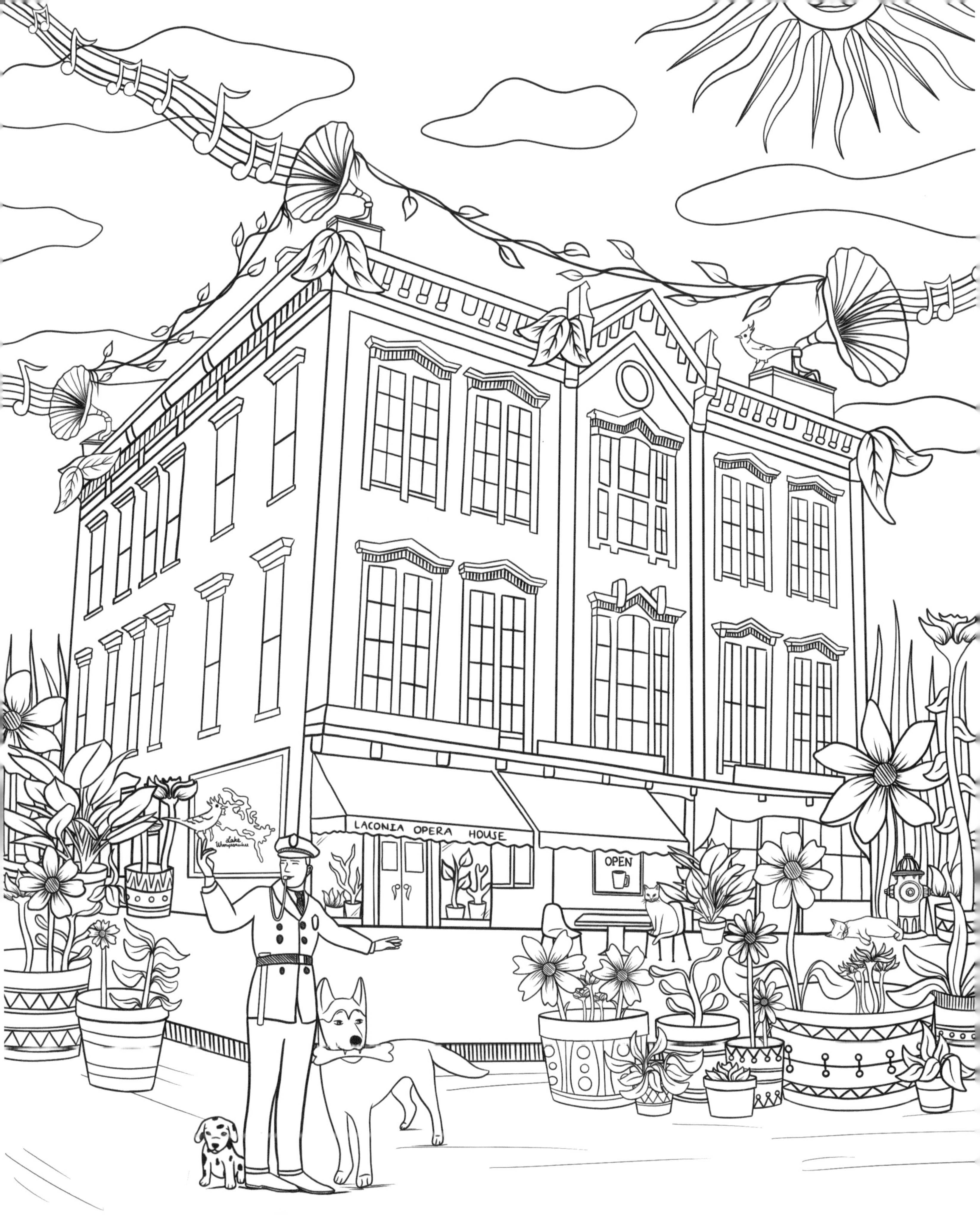

LACONIA OPERA HOUSE
OPEN
Lake Winnipesaukee

Weirs Beach Sign

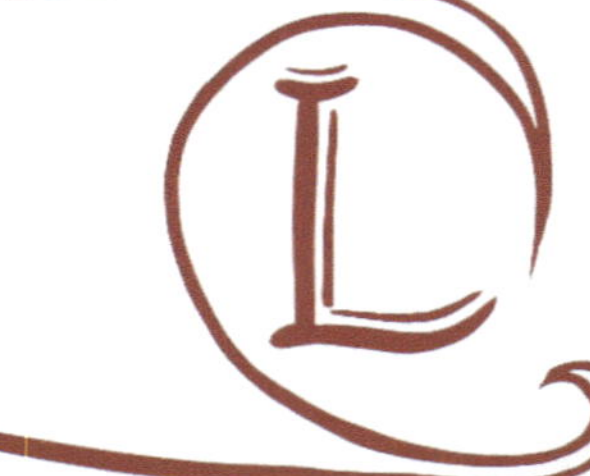

This large neon sentinel welcomes visitors near and far to "The Weirs"—as the locals refer to it.

The sign was erected on Saturday, July 21, 1956, and was the brain child of Sid Ames, local business owner. Ames felt the sign that marked the entrance to Weirs Beach should have the word "Beach" in it. He got together with other businessmen in the area and raised $2000 to have the sign built.

The sign was built by Tyler Advertising Company who modeled it after neon signs the company's owner had seen in Florida. Weighing in at a mere 4400 pounds, its two-sided design beckons visitors to Weirs Beach, the boardwalk, amusement area, and to the Winnipesaukee Flagship Company's MS Mount Washington.

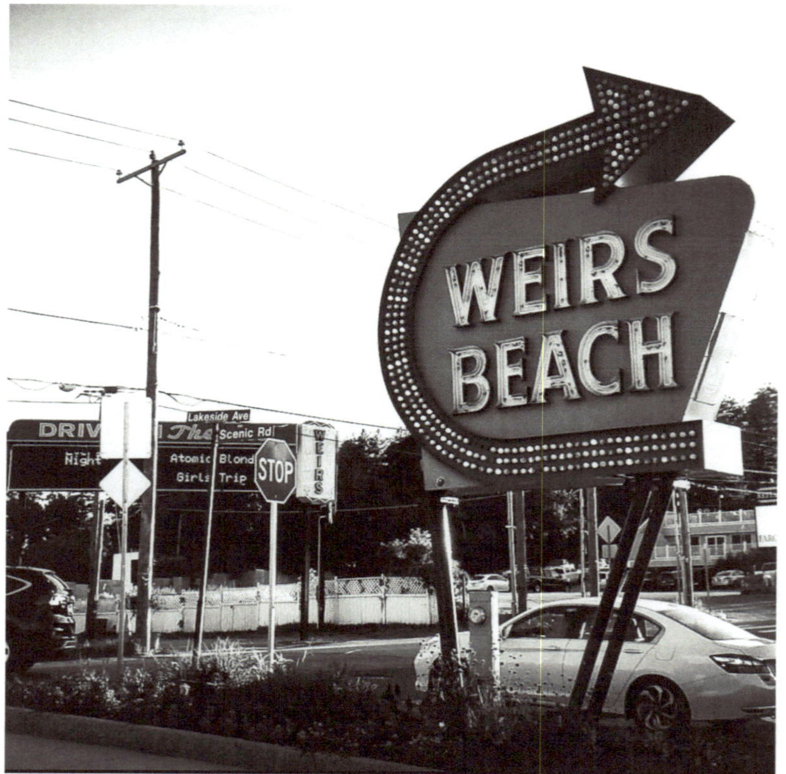

Photograph by BecaLynne Bolen

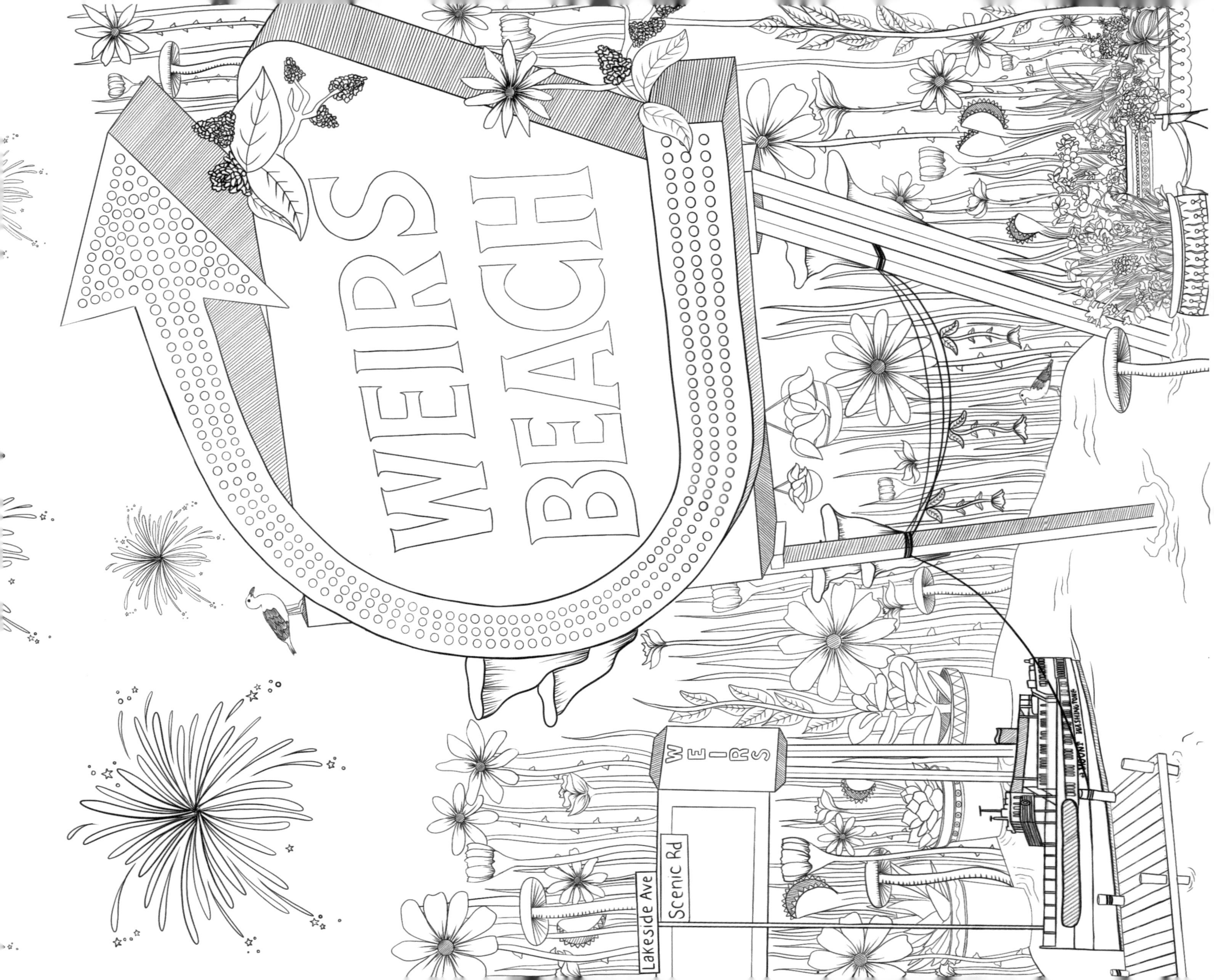

WEIRS BEACH
WEIRS
Lakeside Ave
Scenic Rd

Endicott Rock

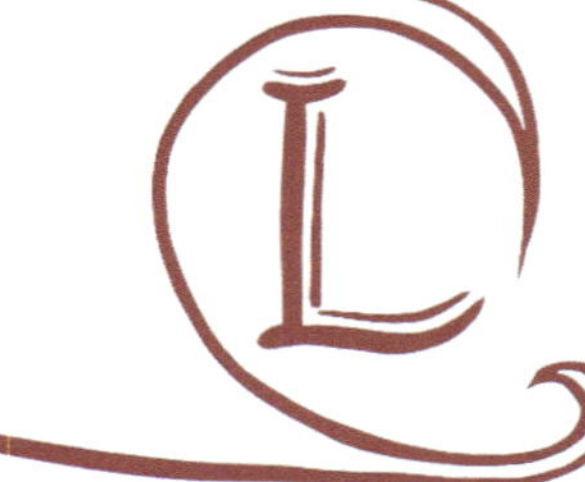

Endicott Rock is one of the oldest artifacts of America's settlement. It marks what was once thought to be the northernmost boundary of the Massachusetts Bay Colony and is a monument to the first white men's visit that left any tangible evidence.

In 1652, a small group of explorers and two native guides were sent by Governor John Endicott to discover the source of the Merrimack River. Upon reaching The Weirs on Lake Winnipesaukee, they inscribed the rock with the governor's name and their own initials.

Later, an English court ruled that the charter of the colony had envisioned the boundary as three miles north of the mouth of the river, where it is today, between Seabrook, NH, and Salisbury, MA.

In 1892, the State of NH built a granite enclosure to protect the rock and the initials that were once carved into it so many years ago. In 1901, a statue of a Native American known as "Captain Jack" was placed atop the monument. Struck by lightning and later severely damaged and thrown into the channel by vandals in 1984, "Captain Jack" was restored by the State and was moved to the Laconia Public Library for safekeeping.

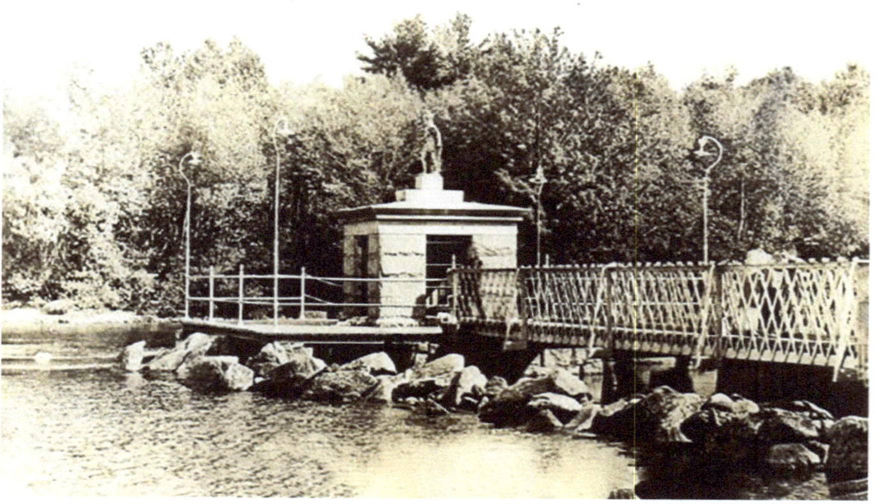

From the Lakes Region History Online Collection

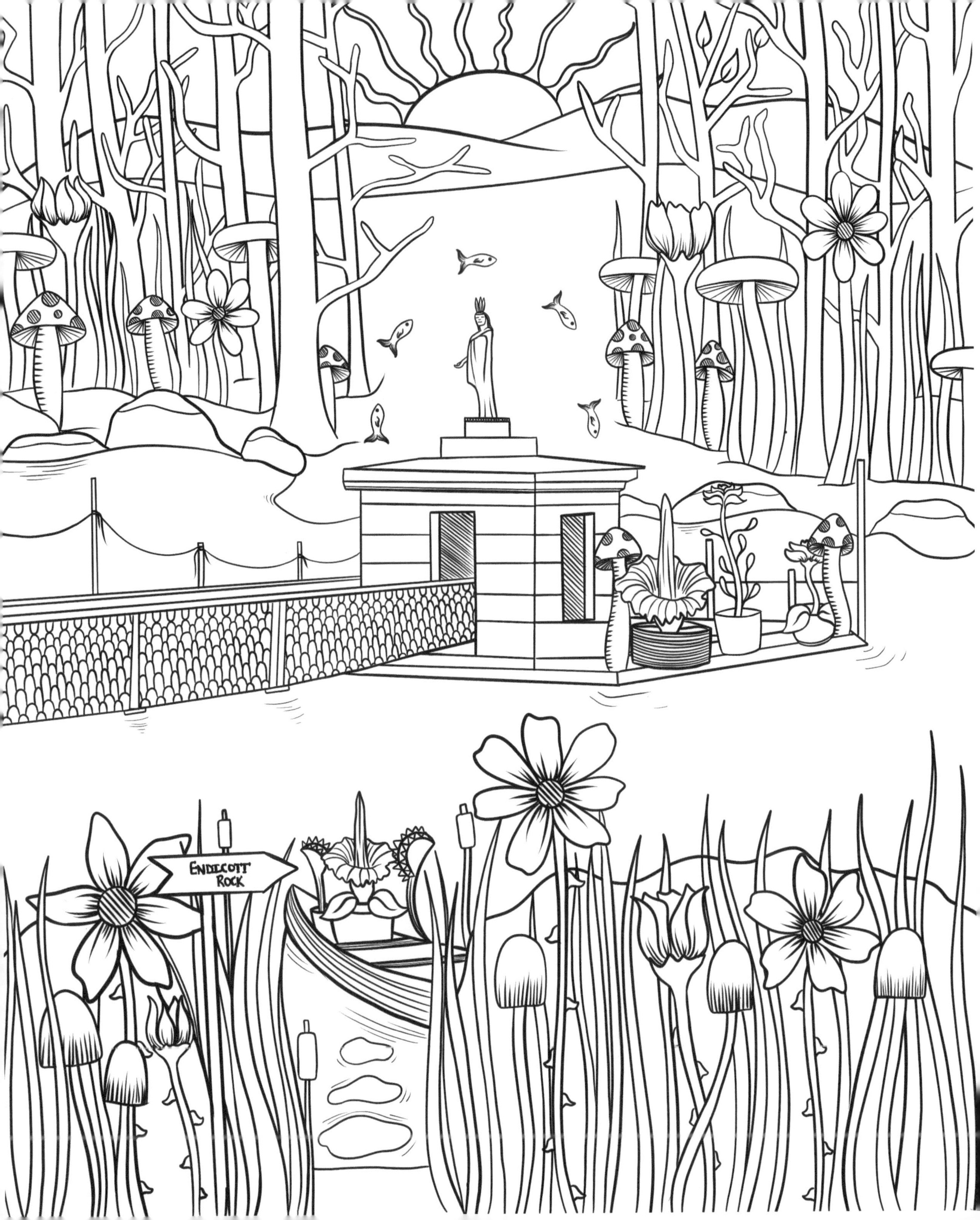

ENDICOTT
ROCK

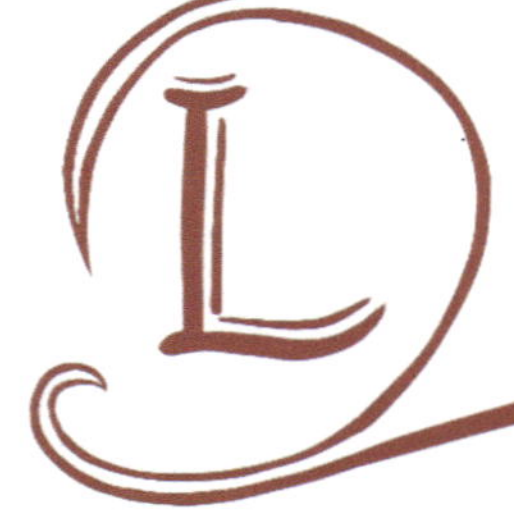

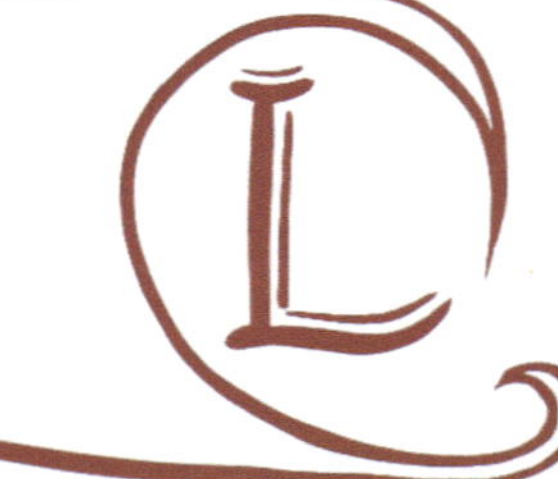

Benjamin Piscopo House

Benjamin Piscopo, the original developer of the Colonial Theatre, emigrated from Italy to Boston, MA, in 1882 at the age of 18.

He first worked in a marble shop, then as a barber and a baker. He was able to save up enough money to start a hotel in Boston, which he originally named Hotel Piscopo but later changed the name to Hotel Florence. He was a successful real estate developer, owning 15 or more large properties.

Piscopo built a home on Lake Winnisquam and spent summers there. Because he loved the area so much, in 1911 he moved to Laconia permanently and built a beautiful home on Pleasant Street.

In Laconia, he developed a number of the city's prominent buildings. In addition to the Colonial Theatre, he built the New Piscopo Block in 1924, purchased the Eagle Hotel, and was the largest investor in, and later sole owner of, The Laconia Tavern.

Fun Fact: At the time of his death in 1926, he was the largest property owner in Laconia.

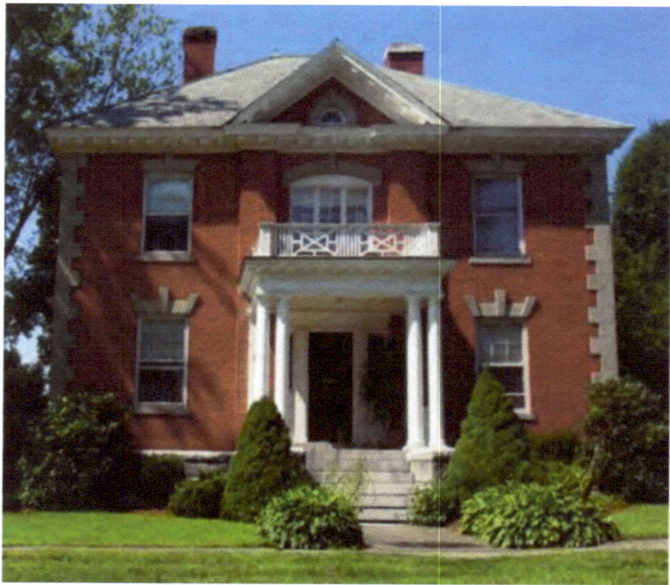

Photograph by Brenda Kean

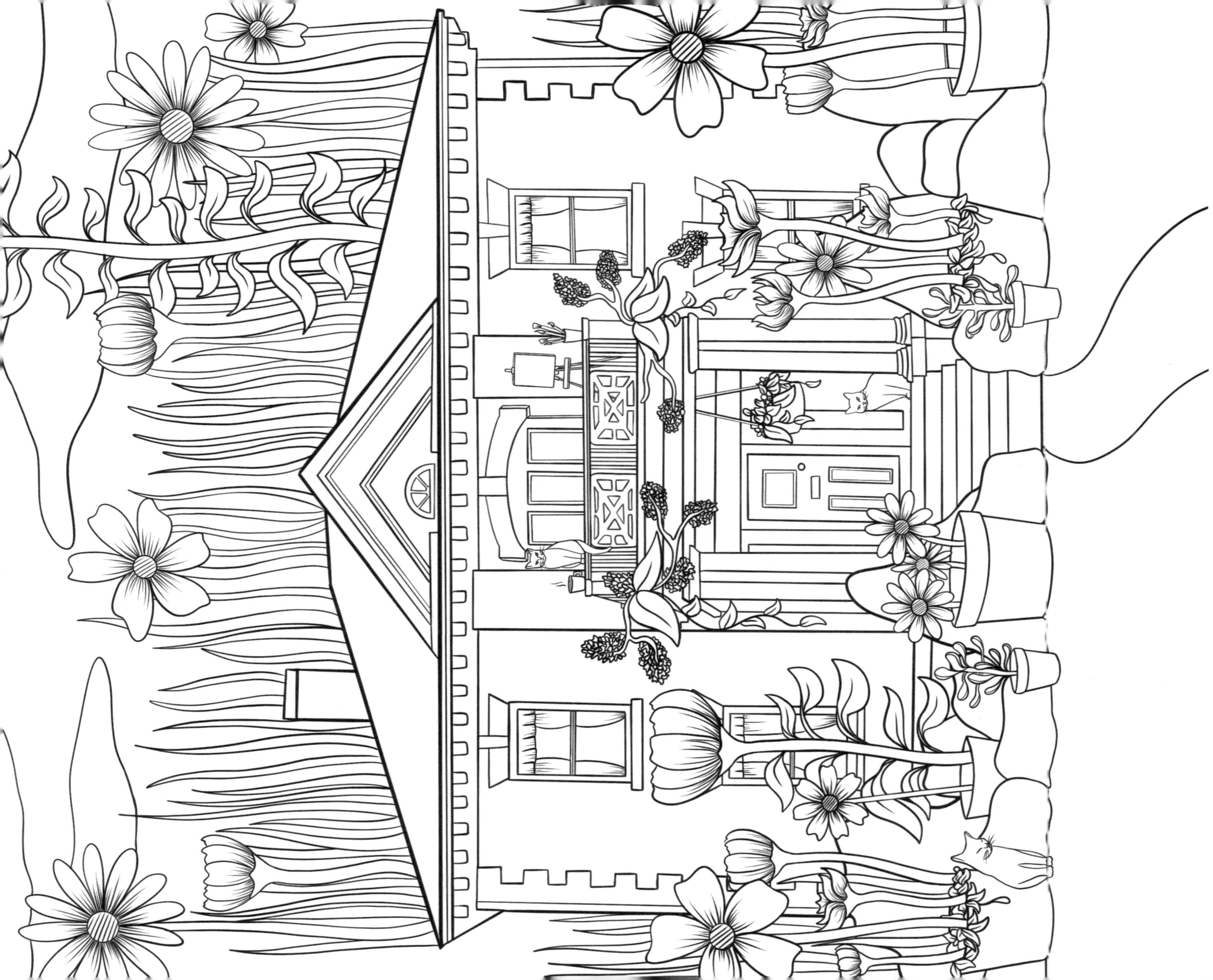

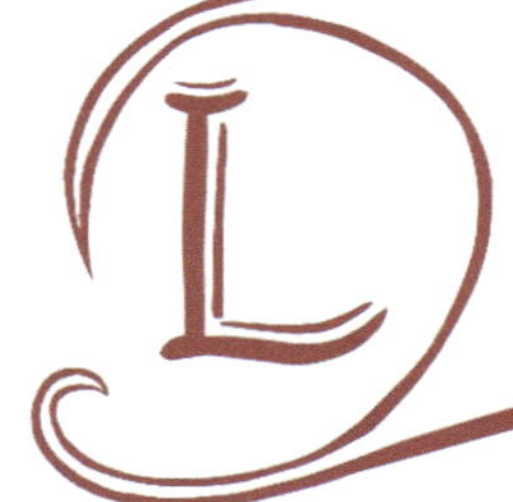

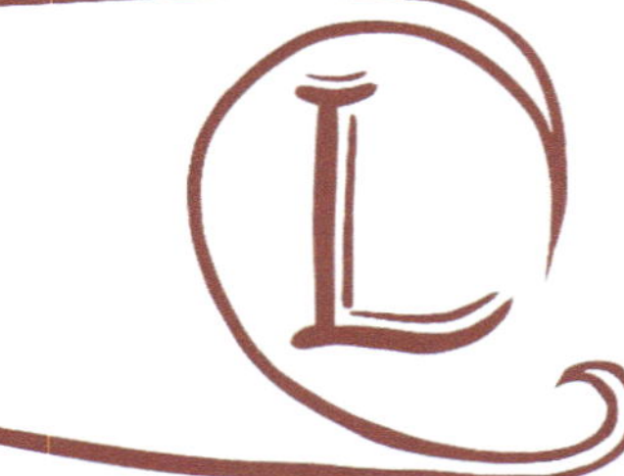

Laconia Water Company

In 1883, a charter was obtained, and in 1894, the Laconia and Lake Village Water-Works was organized by W. L. Melcher and Col. B. F. Drake. The plant was built in 1885 and was in operation by December of that same year.

The company changed its name to Laconia Water Works in 1897. The Hon. John C. Moulton was the first president of the corporation.

The city purchased the Laconia Water Co. and Weirs Water Co. in 1955 for $850,000, establishing a Water Commission to oversee this city department.

Fun Fact: The company started with a capital fund of $60,000.

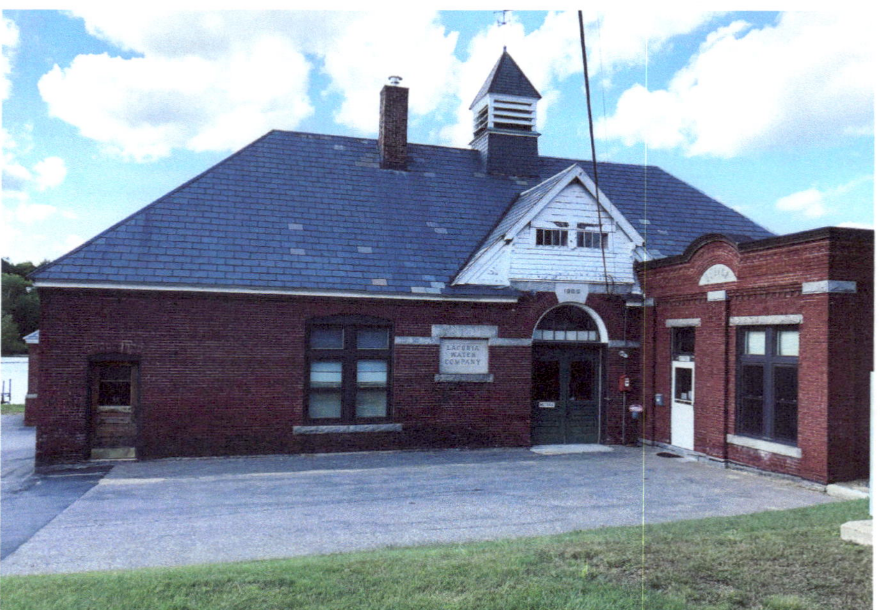

Photograph by Heidi Smith

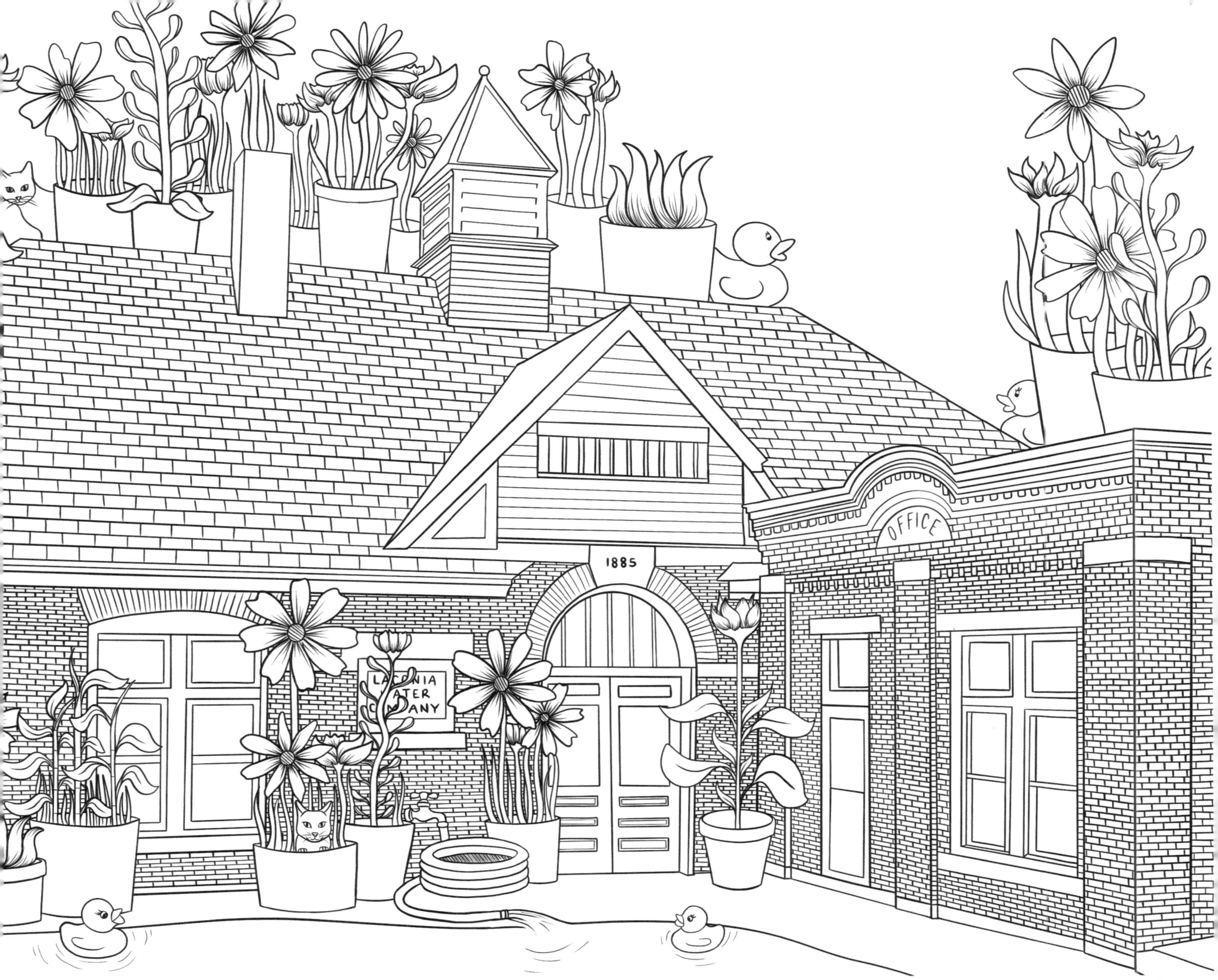

LACONIA WATER COMPANY
1885
OFFICE

Laconia Country Club

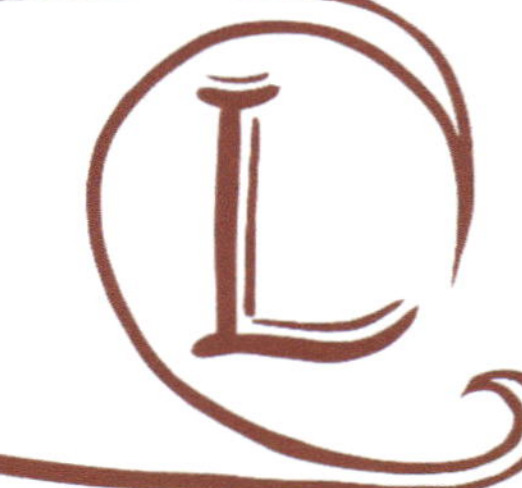

The Laconia Country Club sits on the site that had once been the Herbert Sanborn family dairy farm for 18 years. The Sanborn property went from the shore of Lake Opechee to the shore of what was known as Lake Paugus, now called Paugus Bay.

Joseph Dauphin bought the property from the Sanborn family in 1916 for $11,500. Joseph sold it to the LCC Holding Company in 1921 for $13,500.

The LCC got its official beginning with a meeting at the Laconia Tavern on January 16, 1922. The original incorporators were Harry S. Chase, Edmund Fitzgerald, Charles Hayford and Thomas P. Cheney.

The Sanborn farmhouse was converted into a pro shop but was eventually replaced. The farm's original barn remained on the property and became the original clubhouse of LCC. Unfortunately, it burned down November 9, 1965. April 1966 was the groundbreaking for the new clubhouse.

Fun Fact: In 1928, greens fees were listed at $2.50. In 1984, Ginny Wakeman was elected as the first-ever woman president of the Club. Over the years, several famous people, including Mickey Rooney and Tom Poston, have visited LCC for a game of golf.

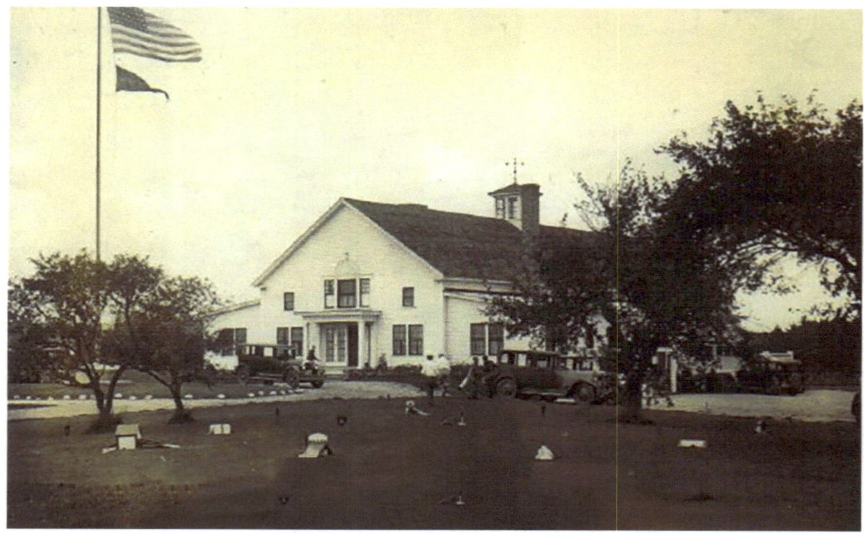

From the Lakes Region History Online Collection

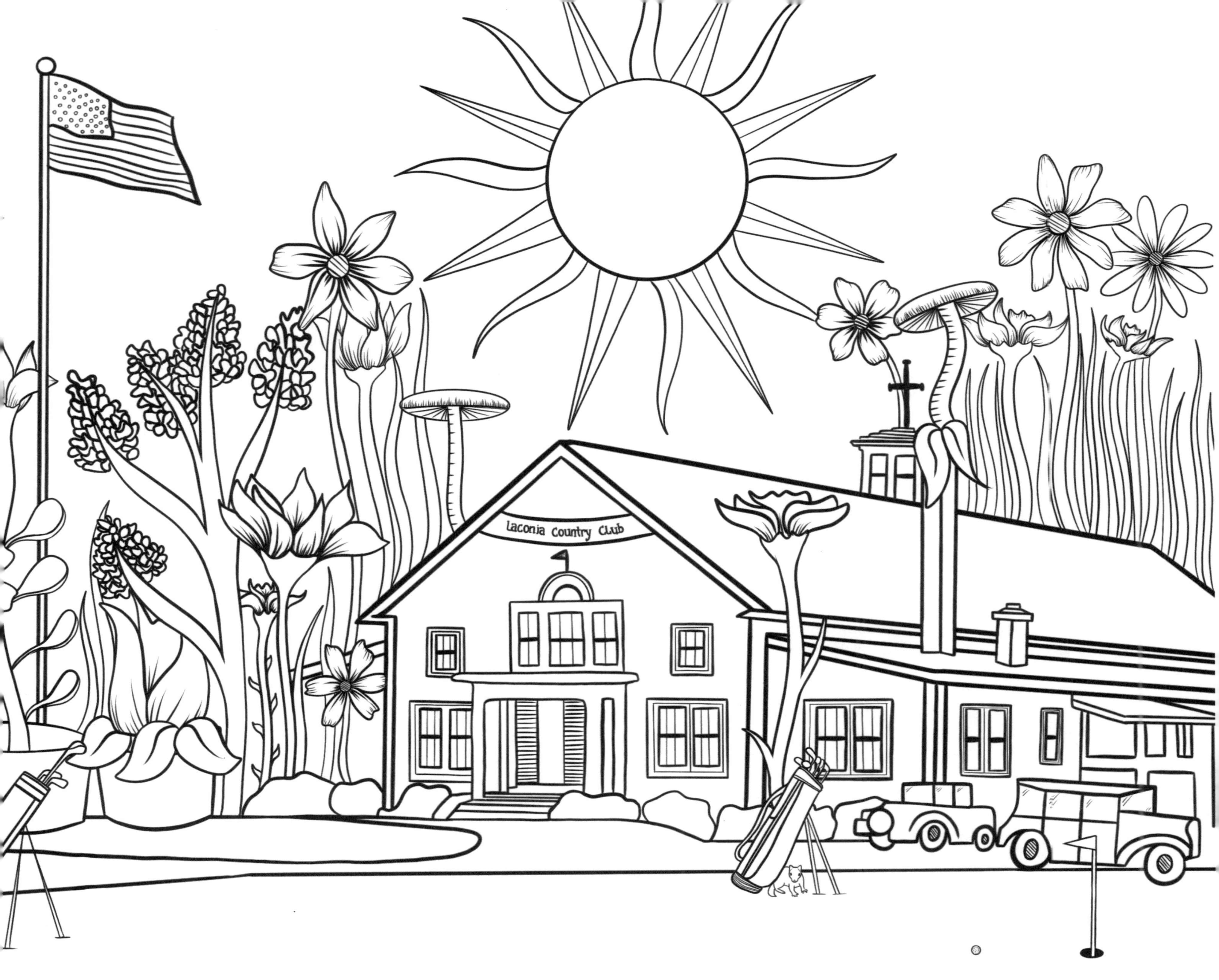

Laconia Country Club

Kellerhaus

Kellerhaus, one of NH's oldest ice cream and candy makers, was originally located on Main Street, Laconia.

In 1906, Otto G. Keller came to Laconia from Merrimack. Practically penniless, he started working at the Phillips' Candy Store on Main Street. A year later, he was able to purchase the store and establish Keller's Confections with Candy and Chocolate.

In 1966 with the urban renewal project, the building where the Keller's store was located was going to be torn down. The Kellers then purchased an estate in The Weirs owned and built by Myron B. Hart and known as Hartland. They relocated to that property and renamed it Kellerhaus.

Through the years, until 1989, generations of Kellers continued to run and work at the store. The current owners, Daryl Dawson and Brian Head, maintain many of the Keller traditions and use some of the original recipes that have been handed down by the Keller family.

Fun Fact: Otto started making homemade ice cream in the early 1920s. Although refrigeration technology was not yet created, he was able to offer it year round by using ice from Lake Winnipesaukee and tons of rock salt.

Seth Keller, Otto's son, created the first ice cream buffet in the area.

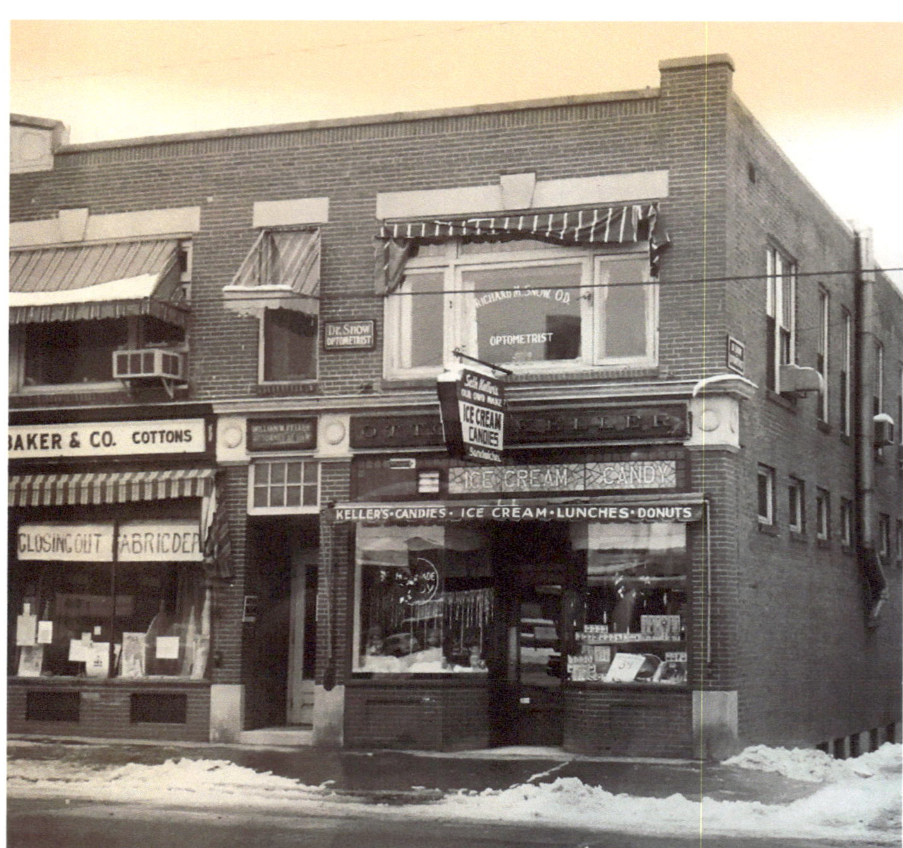

Photograph from Kellerhaus

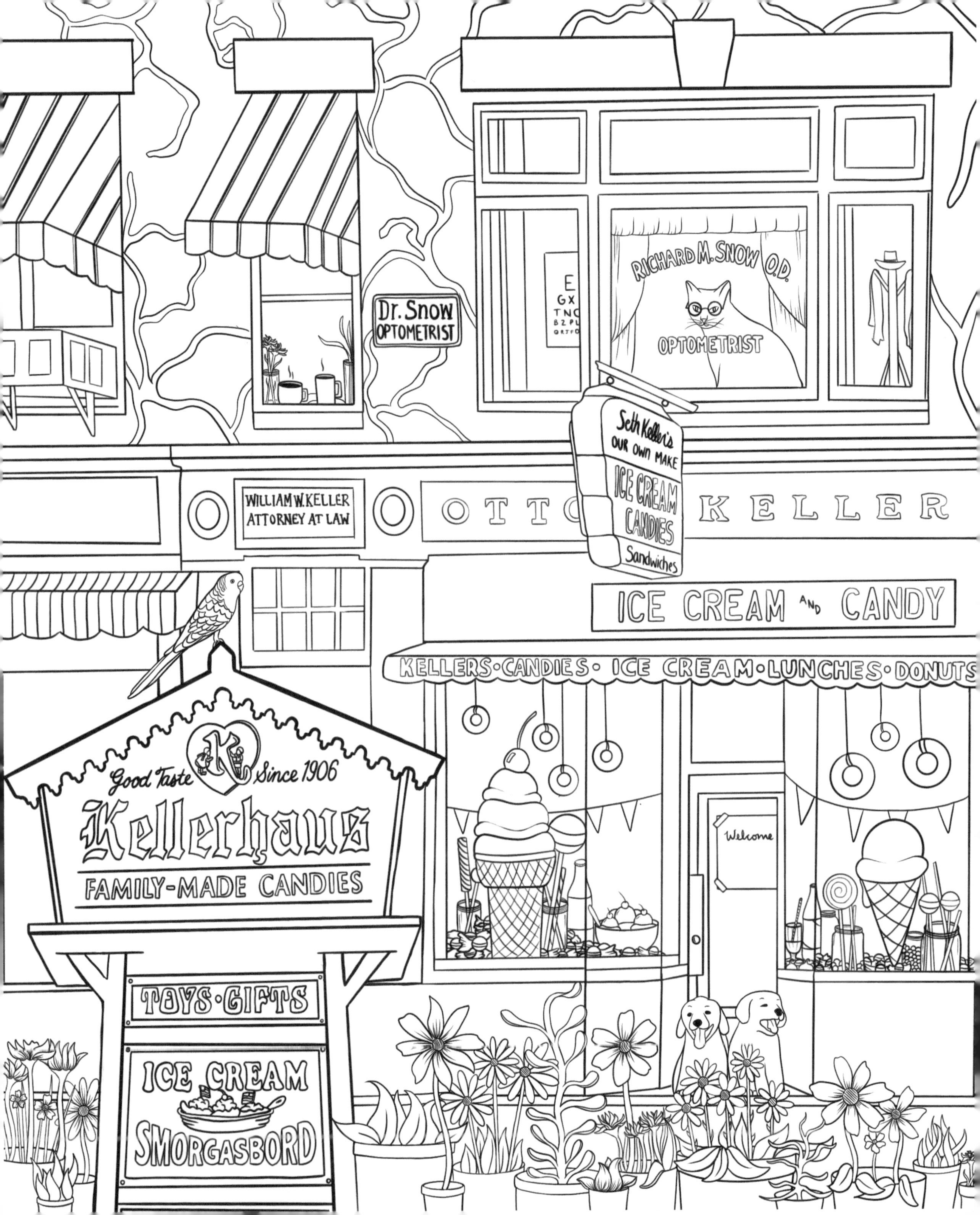
Dr. Snow
OPTOMETRIST
RICHARD M. SNOW O.D.
OPTOMETRIST
E
GX
TNC
B2PL
QRTF
Seth Keller's
OUR OWN MAKE
ICE CREAM
CANDIES
Sandwiches
WILLIAM W. KELLER
ATTORNEY AT LAW
OTTO
KELLER
ICE CREAM AND CANDY
KELLERS·CANDIES·ICE CREAM·LUNCHES·DONUTS
Welcome
Good Taste   Since 1906
Kellerhaus
FAMILY-MADE CANDIES
TOYS·GIFTS
ICE CREAM
SMORGASBORD

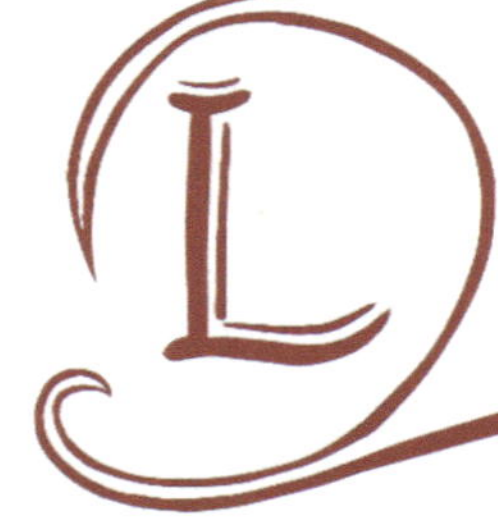

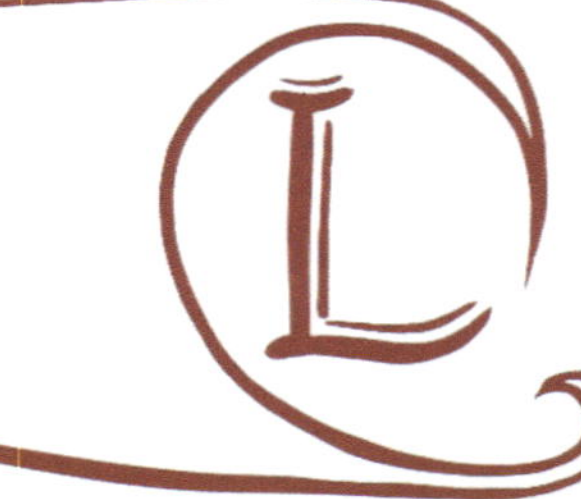

Laconia Car Company

Originally named the Charles Ranlet Car Manufacturing Company, the Laconia Car Company manufactured railway cars in Laconia, NH, from 1848 to 1928. Charles Ranlet, a Gilford native, started the company the same year the railroad reached Meredith Bridge, as Laconia was earlier known.

The company produced thousands of railroad cars, both freight and passenger, and hundreds of trolley and subway cars, the vast majority of which went to rail and trolley lines on the East Coast. The company built at least two coaches for the Mount Washington Cog Railway.

Initially, the bodies of the cars were made of wood but eventually they were made out of steel. The company performed all the various processes necessary to build a coach, from casting of iron and brass, carpentry and cabinetwork, machining, electrical wiring, lights, plumbing, manufacture of seats, upholstery, decoration, glass, painting, varnishing, etc. A bronze "Laconia Car Co." plaque was installed in each of its products.

Fun Fact: Charles's first job was a machinist at the Belknap Mill.

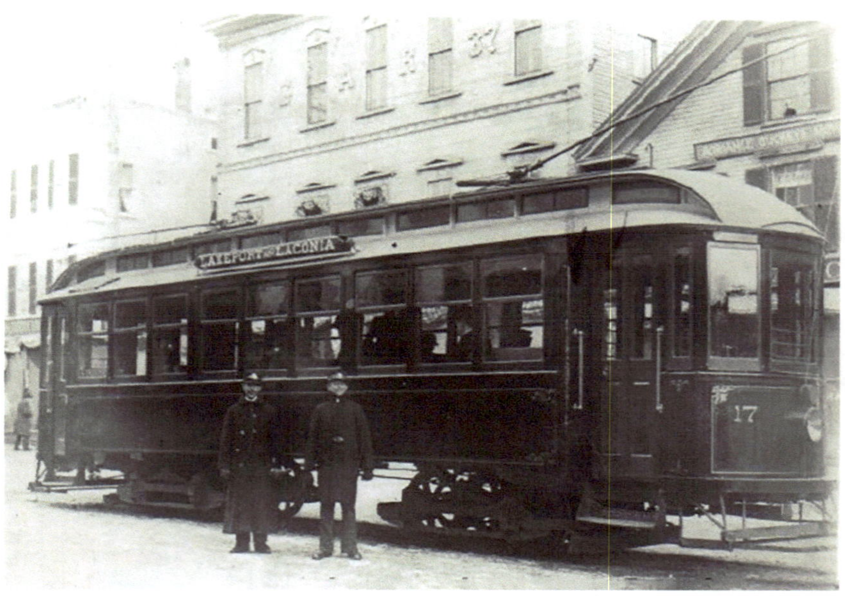

From the Lakes Region History Online Collection

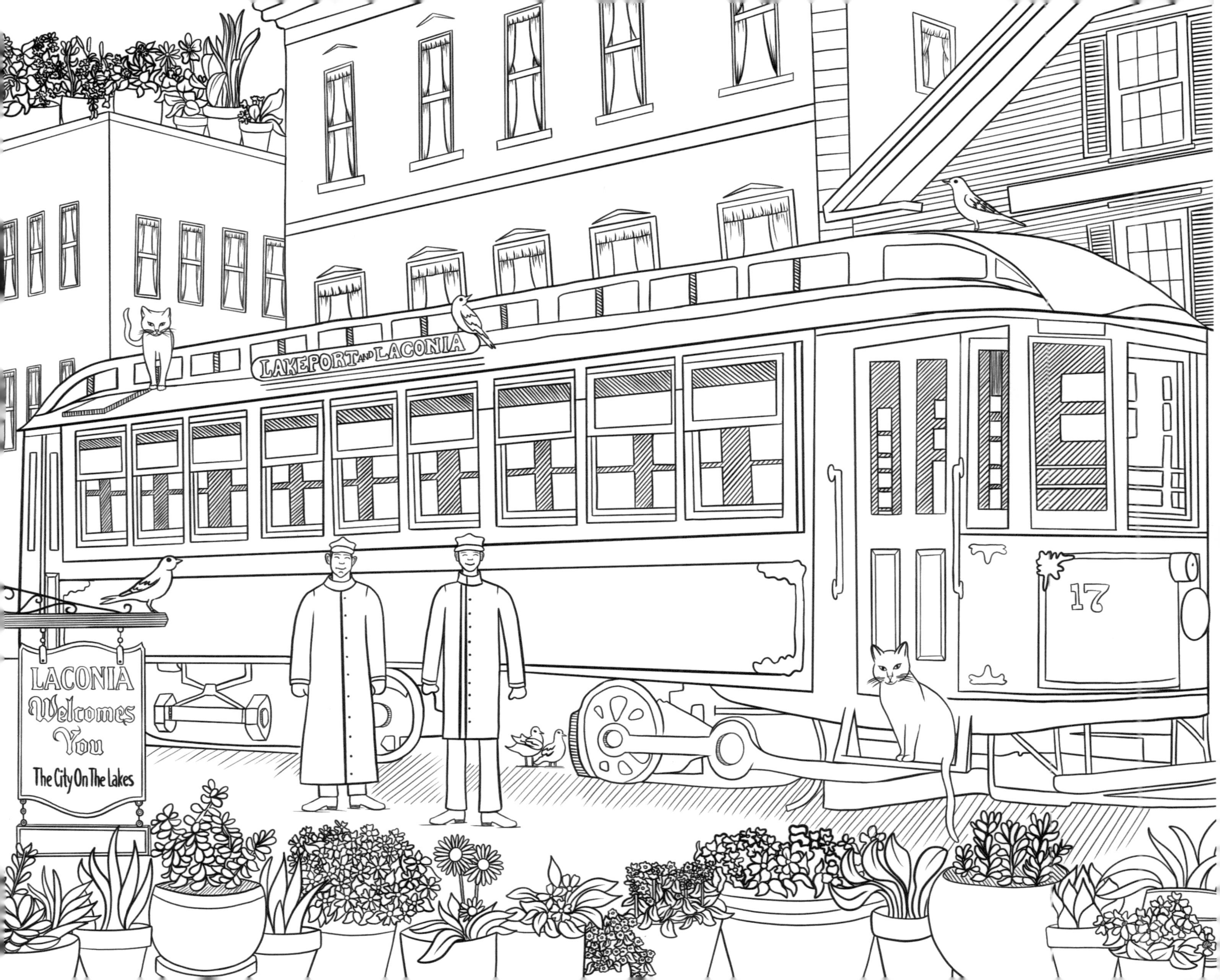

LAKEPORT AND LACONIA
LACONIA
Welcomes
You
The City On The Lakes
17

The Perley Oak

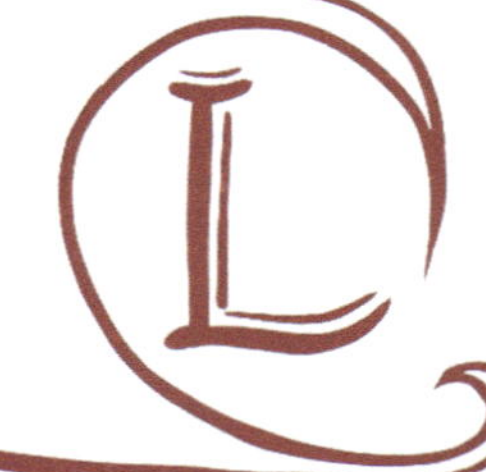

This 400+ year-old state champion prized white oak is located at the Perley Conservation area off of North Main Street.

The oak and the pond were both part of the original Stephen Perley family farm. The farmhouse and barn were located across the street at the corner of Old North Main and North Main. To the right of the tree was a hay barn which was built by John L Perley Sr., resident and one of the founders of Laconia Savings Bank, in 1843. The barn was torn down in 1960.

The Perley family deeded the area, which included the pond and the oak, to the city to be managed by the Conservation Commission. The deed gave explicit instructions regarding the maintenance requirements of the oak and the pond so that future generations could come and enjoy the area.

Fun Fact: The oak was at one time in jeopardy of having to be cut down because of its fragile state. After many meetings and advice from experts, a decision was reached that although this old fella was indeed dying, there was no reason to take it down.

To this day the oak still stands watch over the pond and the citizens of Laconia where it will remain through the end of its natural life.

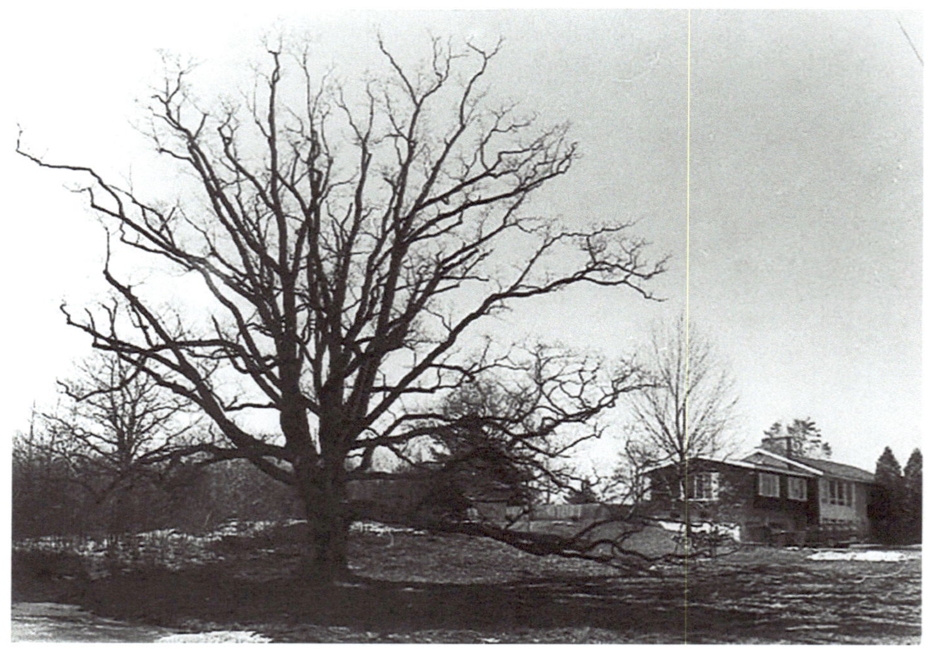

From the Lakes Region History Online Collection

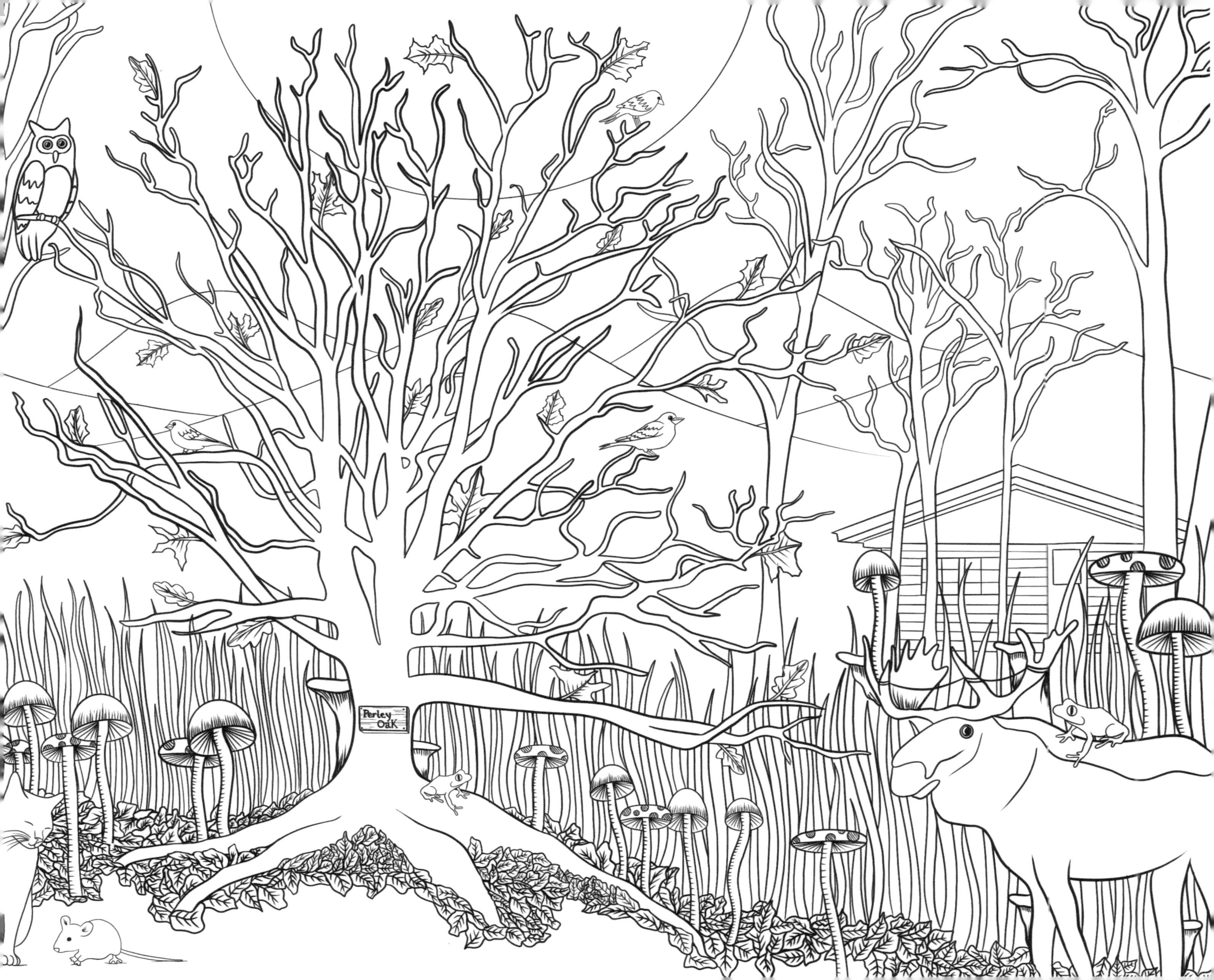
Perley Oak

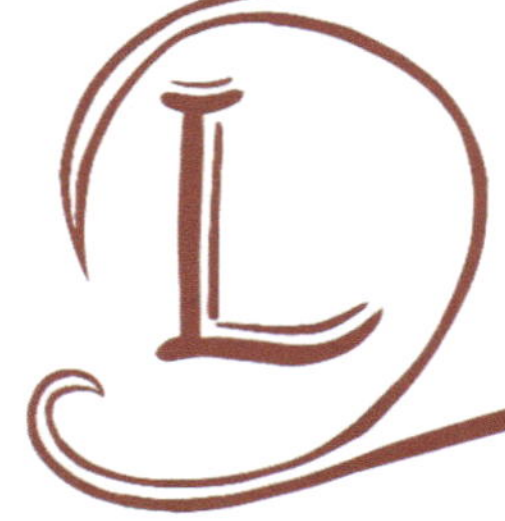

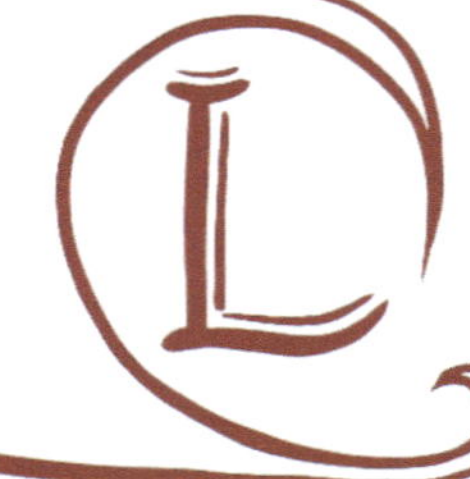

Round Bay Cemetery

Round Bay Cemetery is arguably the oldest cemetery in Laconia. It is located on what was once the land of Ebenezer Smith. He was the first settler in this area and is referred to as "The Father of the Town."

The cemetery likely began as a family burial ground for Smith's family but was later used as a public burial ground for the residents of this area. It has been known as The Smith Yard, Opechee Yard, and later, Round Bay Cemetery.

The oldest grave is that of Susan (or Susannah) Lawrence who died 19 March 1804. She was the daughter of Ebenezer and Sarah (Spiller) Smith and wife of Maj. Samuel Lawrence. Ebenezer and Sarah (Spiller) Smith both died in 1807 within months of each other and are buried here. Their son, Washington Blair Smith, is also buried here; he died in 1855 of injuries sustained in the "Great Catastrophe," when the floor of the new town hall in Meredith collapsed.

Fun Fact: In the fall of 2021, several members of the Laconia Historical and Museum Society along with folks from the NH Old Graveyard Association spent the morning cleaning Ebenezer's and Sarah's headstones. Ebenezer's stone was so taken over by lichen that the epitaph was indecipherable.

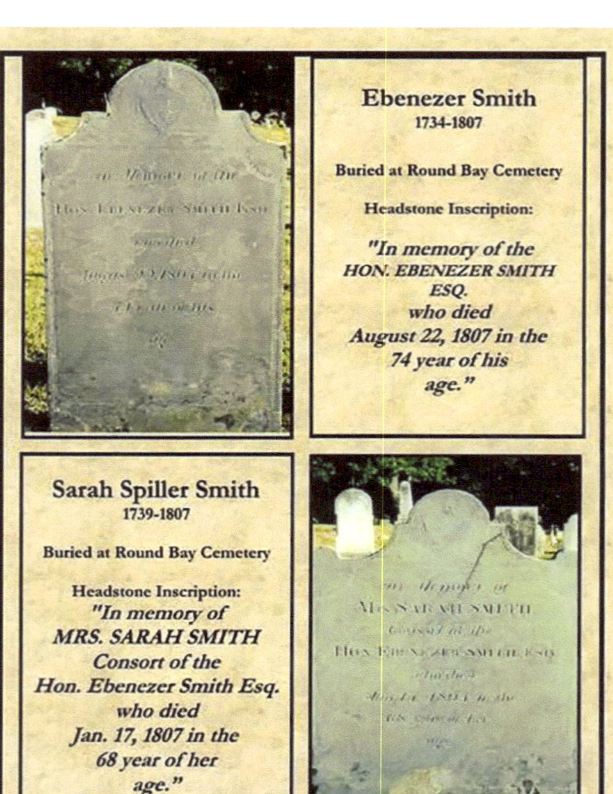

Ebenezer Smith
1734-1807

Buried at Round Bay Cemetery

Headstone Inscription:

"In memory of the
HON. EBENEZER SMITH
ESQ.
who died
August 22, 1807 in the
74 year of his
age."

Sarah Spiller Smith
1739-1807

Buried at Round Bay Cemetery

Headstone Inscription:
"In memory of
MRS. SARAH SMITH
Consort of the
Hon. Ebenezer Smith Esq.
who died
Jan. 17, 1807 in the
68 year of her
age."

Source: Hebert, David. "Ebenezer Smith (1733-1807) - Find A Grave..." Find a Grave, 14 Apr. 2008, www.findagrave.com/memorial/29040019/ebenezer-smith Save.

Laconia Historical and Museum Society

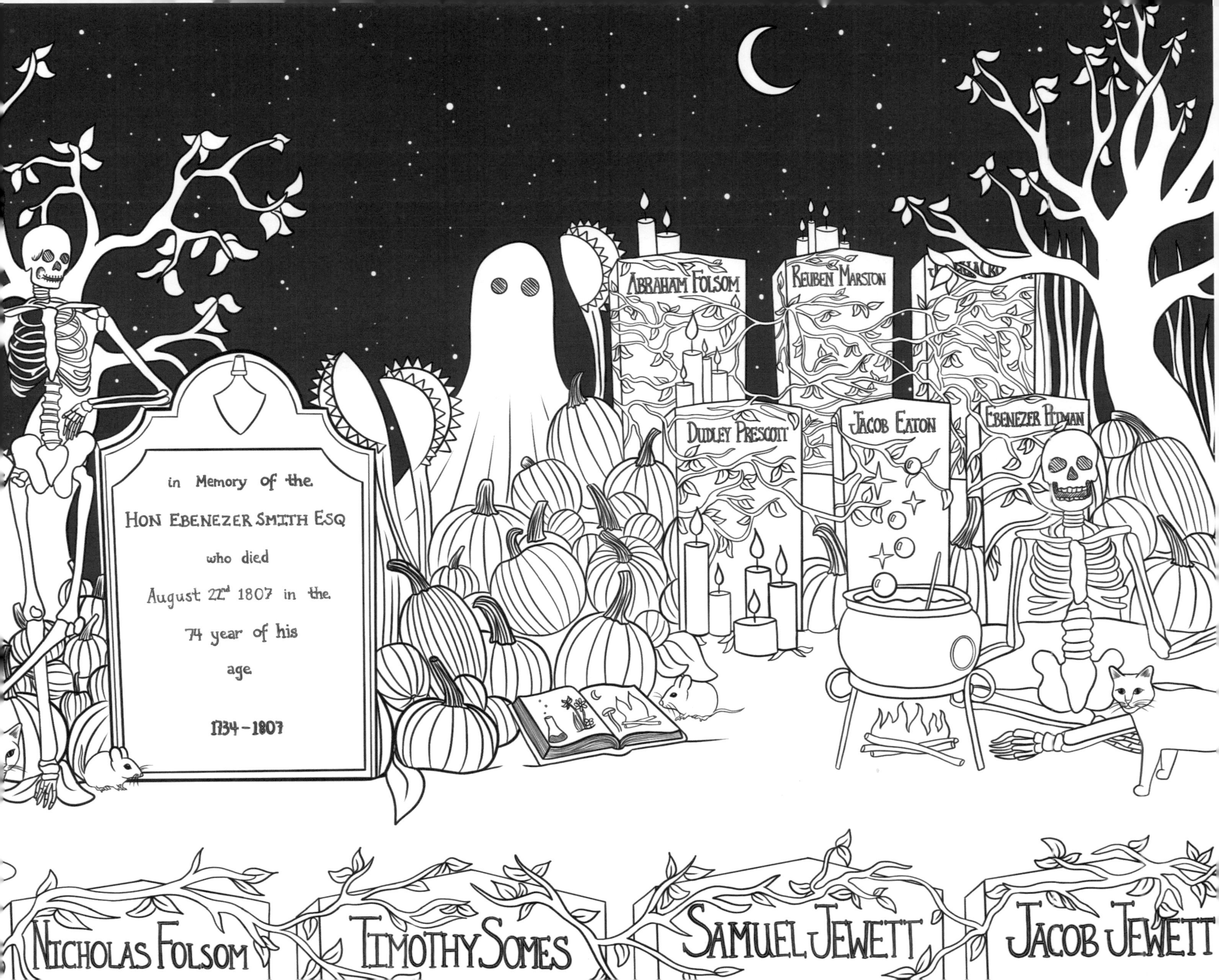

ABRAHAM FOLSOM
REUBEN MARSTON
DUDLEY PRESCOTT
JACOB EATON
EBENEZER PITMAN
in Memory of the
HON EBENEZER SMITH ESQ
who died
August 22nd 1807 in the
74 year of his
age
1734 - 1807
NICHOLAS FOLSOM
TIMOTHY SOMES
SAMUEL JEWETT
JACOB JEWETT

Laconia Hospital

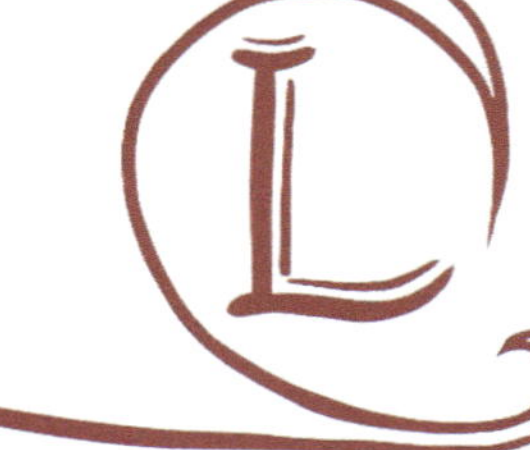

Laconia resident Rhoda C. Ladd of Court Street left her estate, including her home, to the town, suggesting it open its first hospital. Several years after her death (Dec. 21, 1892), Rhoda's former 118 Court Street home was opened on July 19, 1898, as a cottage hospital with a mission to provide quality incare to anyone in need. The hospital had the capacity to hold six to eight patients at a time.

With the town needing a bigger hospital, The Rev. Jeremiah S. Jewett sold his family's farmland on what was then called Jewett Hill to the Laconia Hospital Association in 1905 for $6,000 and donated $3,000 back to help with building the hospital. The cottage hospital relocated to Elliott Street, Oct. 18, 1908, and was renamed Laconia Hospital.

While fund raising was going on to open the first hospital in Laconia, a tragic incident happened in town that confirmed the immediate need for a hospital. On September 1, 1897, at the Messer Street railroad crossing, known then as "Nichols Crossing,"

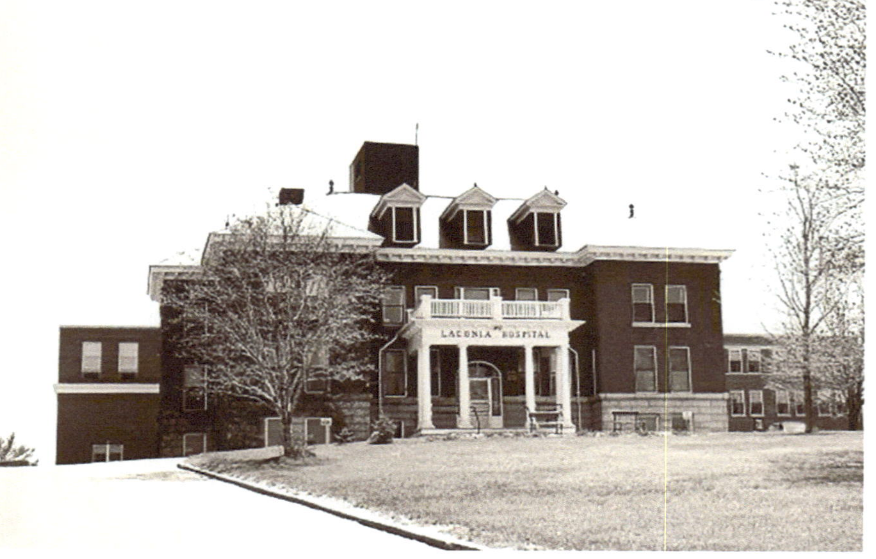

From the Lakes Region History Online Collection

Frank W. Clay and Minnie B. Johnson, both of Laconia, were out for a drive in Clay's horse and carriage. Their carriage was struck by the 7:45 pm Lake Shore train. It was reported that upon impact, the couple was thrown a hundred feet and the horse fifty feet. The frightened horse ran off after tearing itself away from the harness. It took a half hour to transport Clay and Johnson to Mount Belknap Hotel in Lakeport where they waited for the doctors to arrive. Johnson died; Clay recovered.

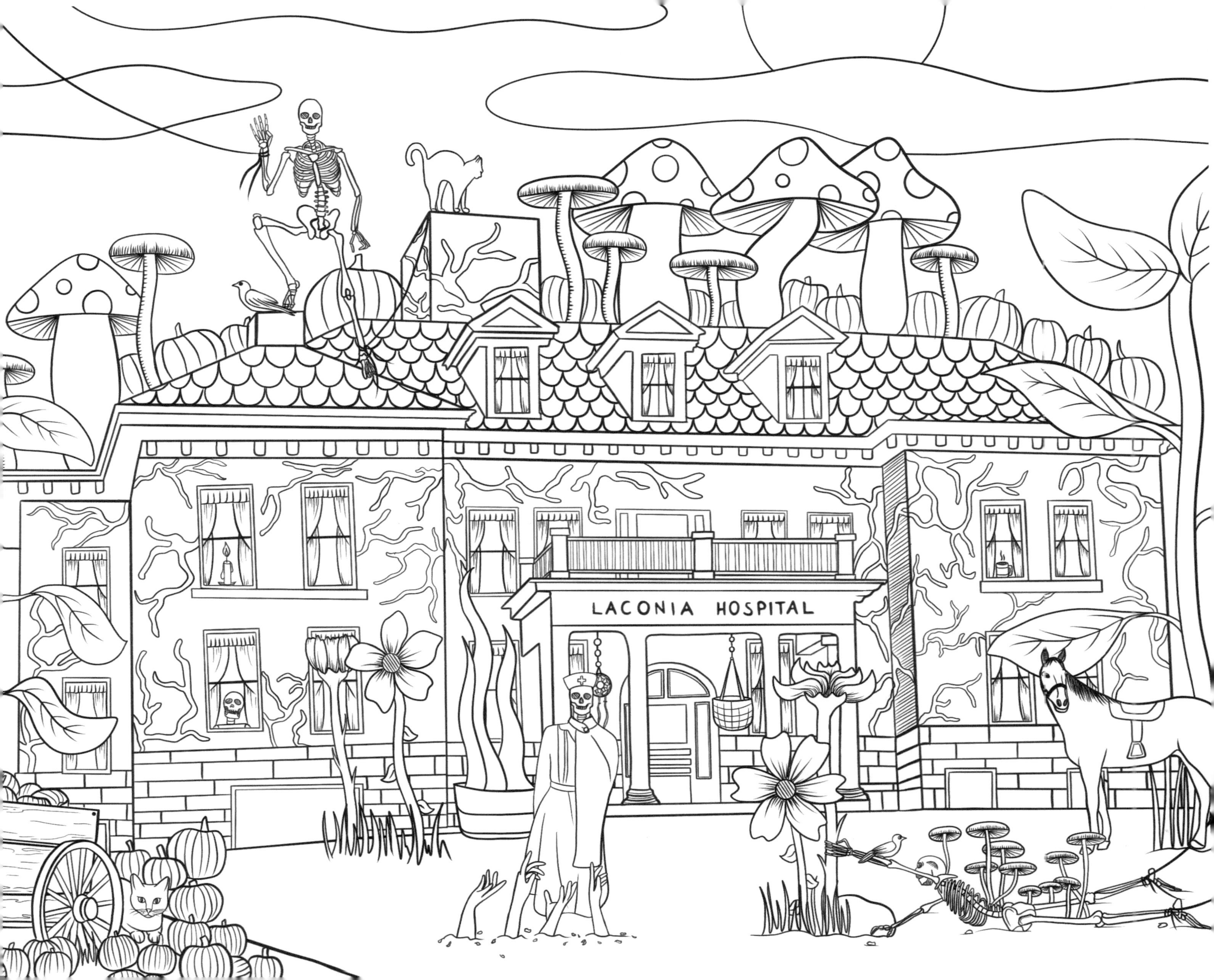

LACONIA HOSPITAL

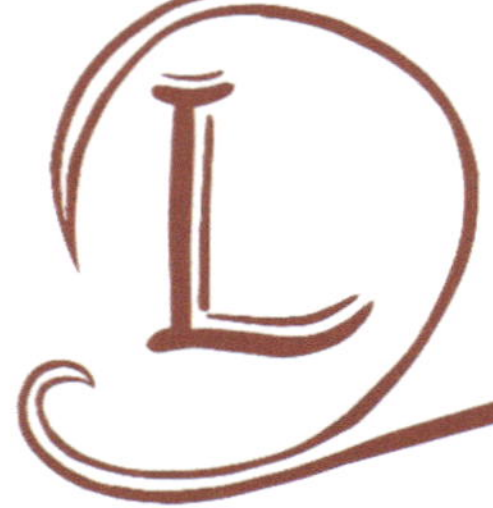

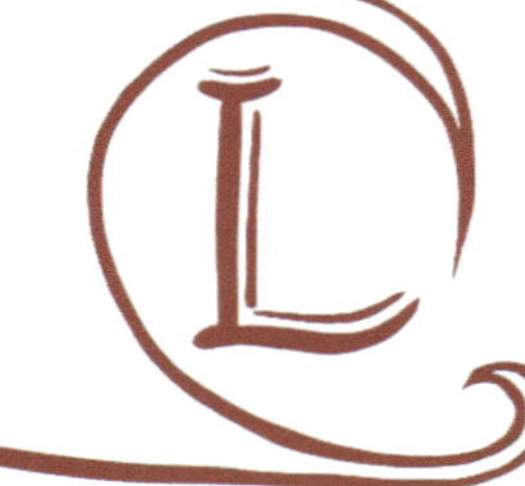

Gove Mansion (around 1890)

Richard Gove, a very wealthy jeweler in the town, built this brick mansion between the Winnipesaukee River and Orange Court. The structure is still standing today.

The automobile (at the lower left) was called the "Fairy Queen" and was one of the first motor carriages in the United States. This steam-powered vehicle was constructed in 1873 by Enos M. Clough, an expert mechanic in the shops of the Boston, Concord & Montreal Railroad in Lakeport. Though moderately successful, the vehicle was "merely a matter of amusement" to its inventor and was abandoned "because it frightened horses."

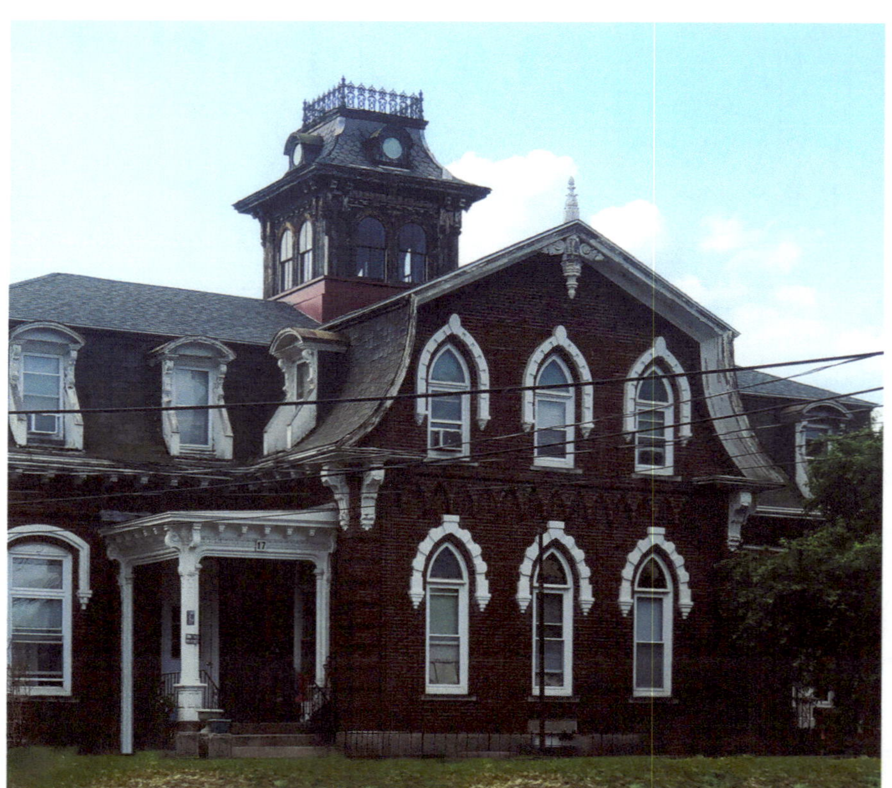

Photo courtesy Heidi Smith

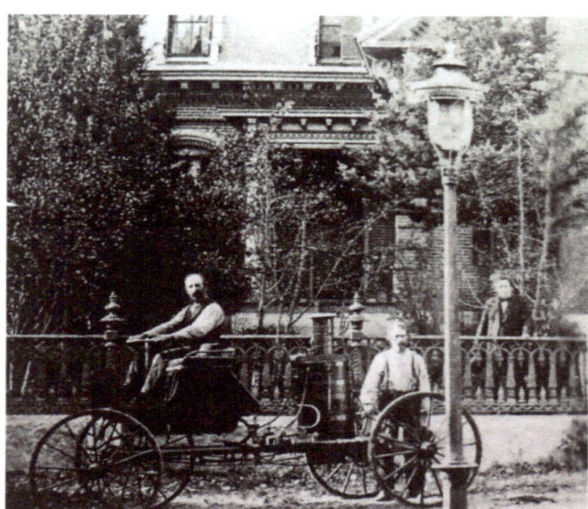

Photo from the Lakes Region History Online Collection

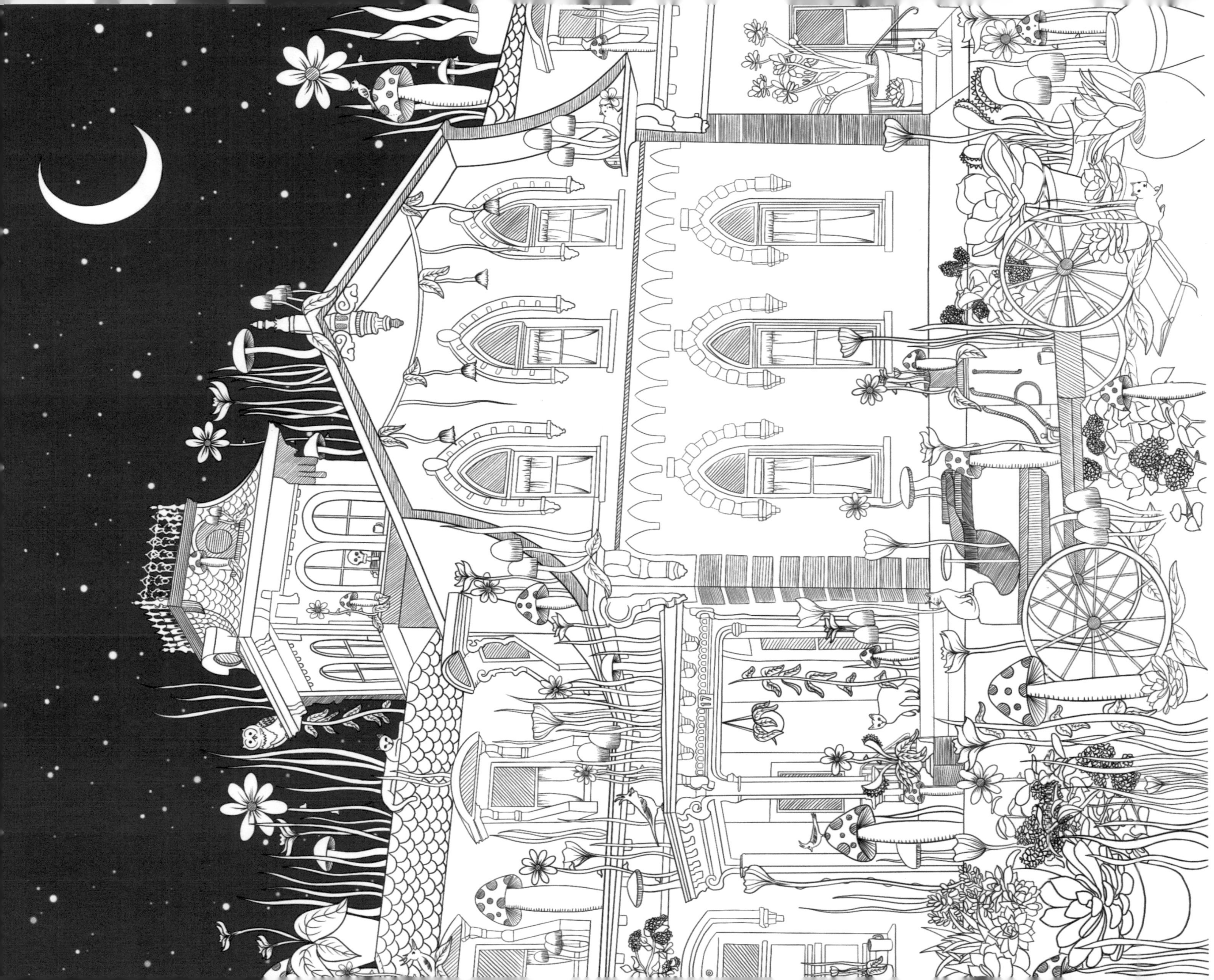

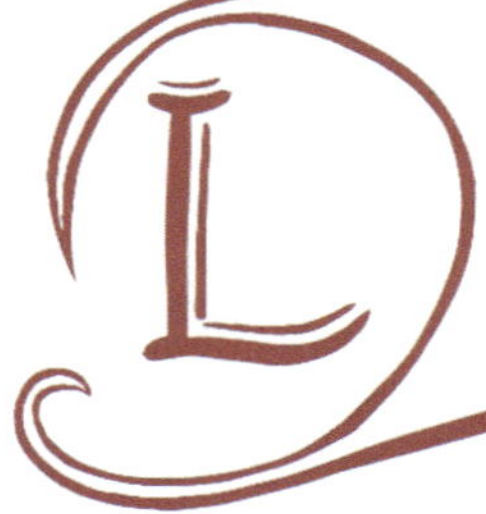
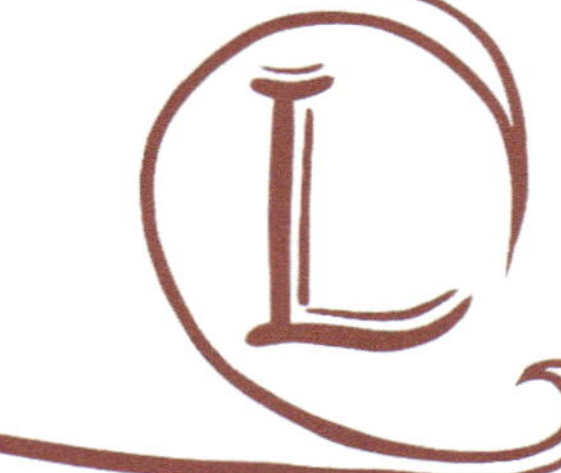

Christmas Village

As busy as Santa, Mrs. Claus and all their elves are during the Christmas season, they have always made time to visit the local children of Laconia at Christmas Village, until the Covid 19 pandemic intervened.

This local tradition began in 1975 by Dick Tapply, city recreation director, who wanted to start a free Christmas celebration for the local children. (Tapply's father, Wink Tapply, had originated a similar "Santa's Workshop" in Bristol.) Bob Hamel, a member of the Jaycees at the time and later a city councilor, heard about Tapply's celebration and helped put on the first Christmas Village.

Eventually Twinkle and Tinsel, aka the Bolduc brothers, Armand and Ernie, joined forces with their friend, Bob Hamel, and went on to manage Christmas Village for years.

Christmas Village, a magical Christmas Wonderland, has brought smiles to the faces of children and adults alike. The kids played games, enjoyed cookies and milk, got to ride on Santa's sleigh, built a wooden ornament they could take home and hang on their tree and enjoyed other activities while they waited to have their own special moment with Santa and have their picture taken with him.

Fun Fact: Every year, someone was named honorary mayor of Christmas Village and presented with a key to the city.

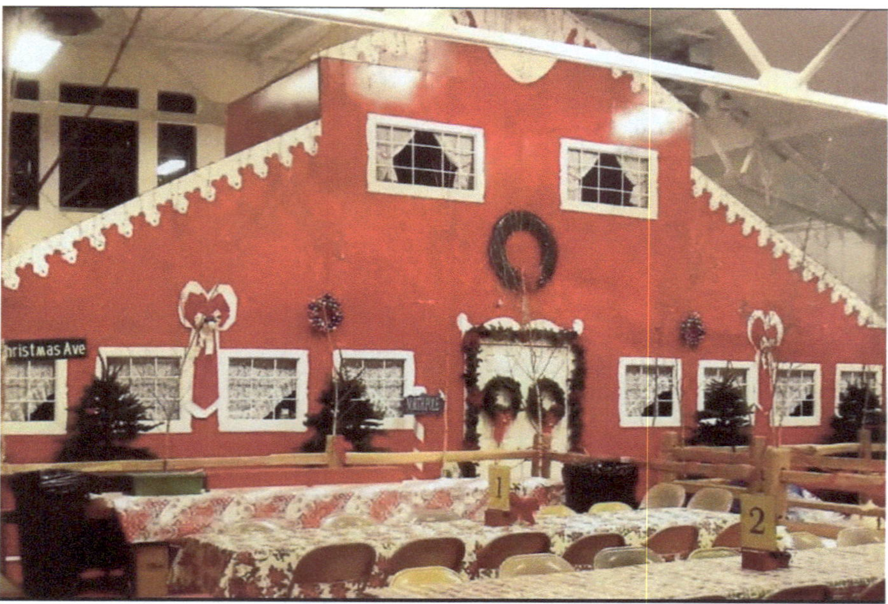

Photo by Ernie Bolduc

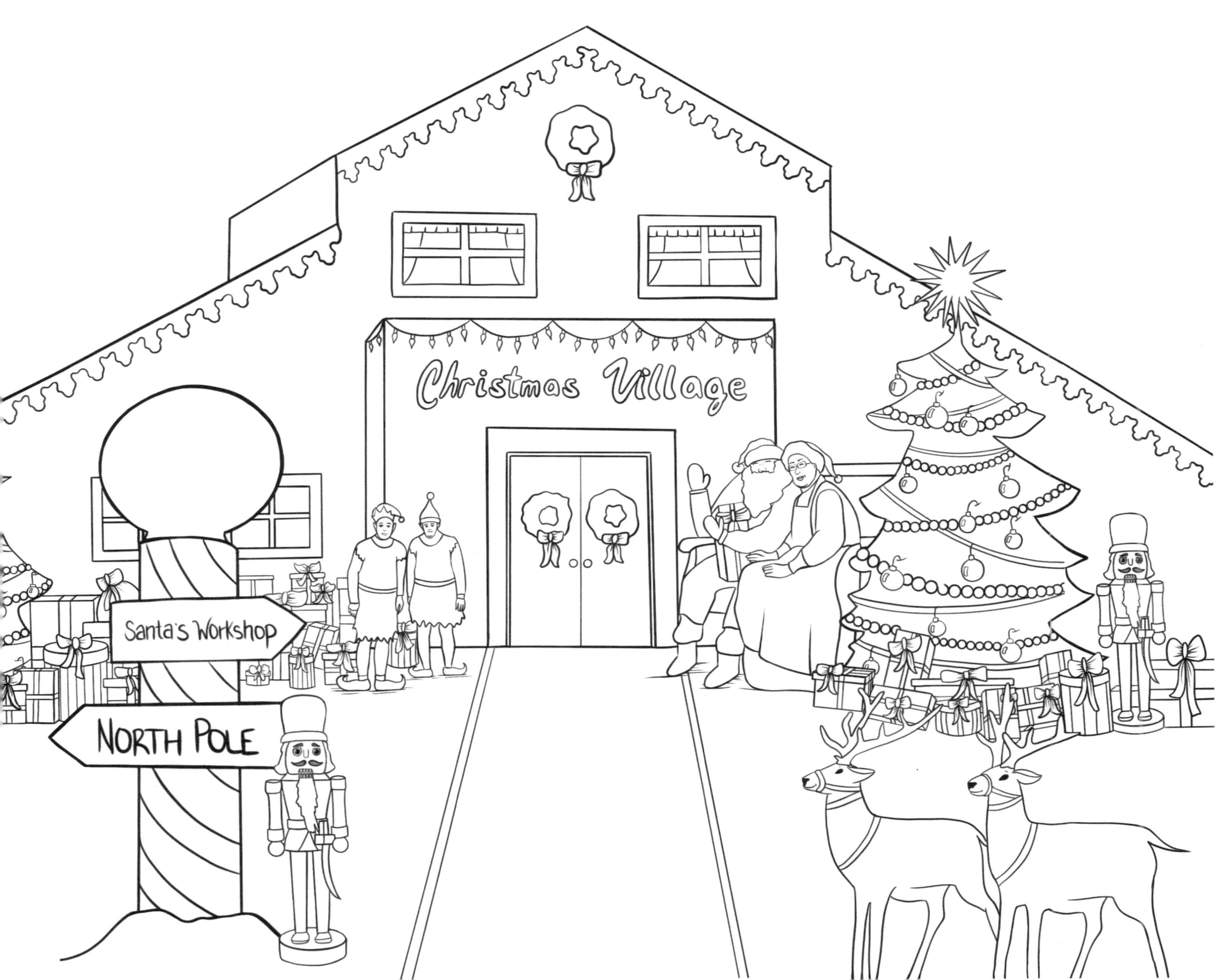

Christmas Village
Santa's Workshop
NORTH POLE

Courtney Parsons

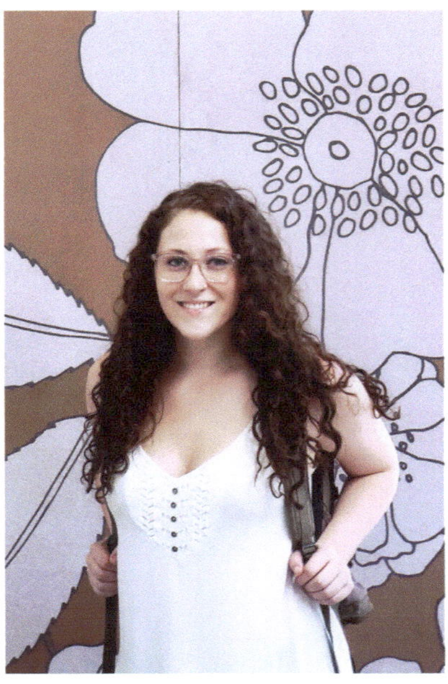

Courtney Parsons was born and raised in Laconia and has a deep love and appreciation for the beauty of the Lakes Region. The illustrations she created for this coloring book draw inspiration from nature and her upbringing in New Hampshire. They are intended to represent the growth and progress over time in our beloved historical city. Courtney currently lives in Northern Virginia and is steadily working towards her bachelor's degree at George Mason University, where she is an art and visual technology student. She considers it an honor to be involved in this project.

Heidi Smith

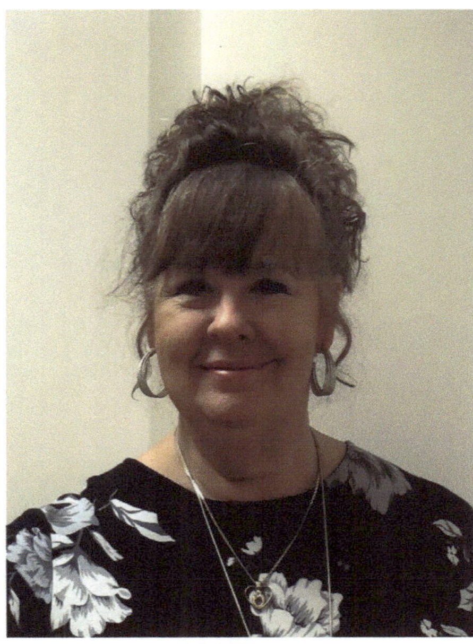

Heidi Smith is a native of the Lakes Region and raised her son here. She has spent the majority of her professional career in the local health care setting, celebrating 36 years.

An avid volunteer with a passion for history, Heidi is currently the Chair of the Laconia Historical and Museum Society (LHMS) Programming Committee and is on the LHMS Board. She brings a key skill set of innovative brainstorming while generating overall LHMS awareness. She enjoys offering various opportunities to the Society, including this unique coloring book. One glimpse at Courtney Parsons' drawing of the Colonial Theatre and she knew this project was the perfect avenue to bring a fun and engaging version of the City of Laconia's history into every household.

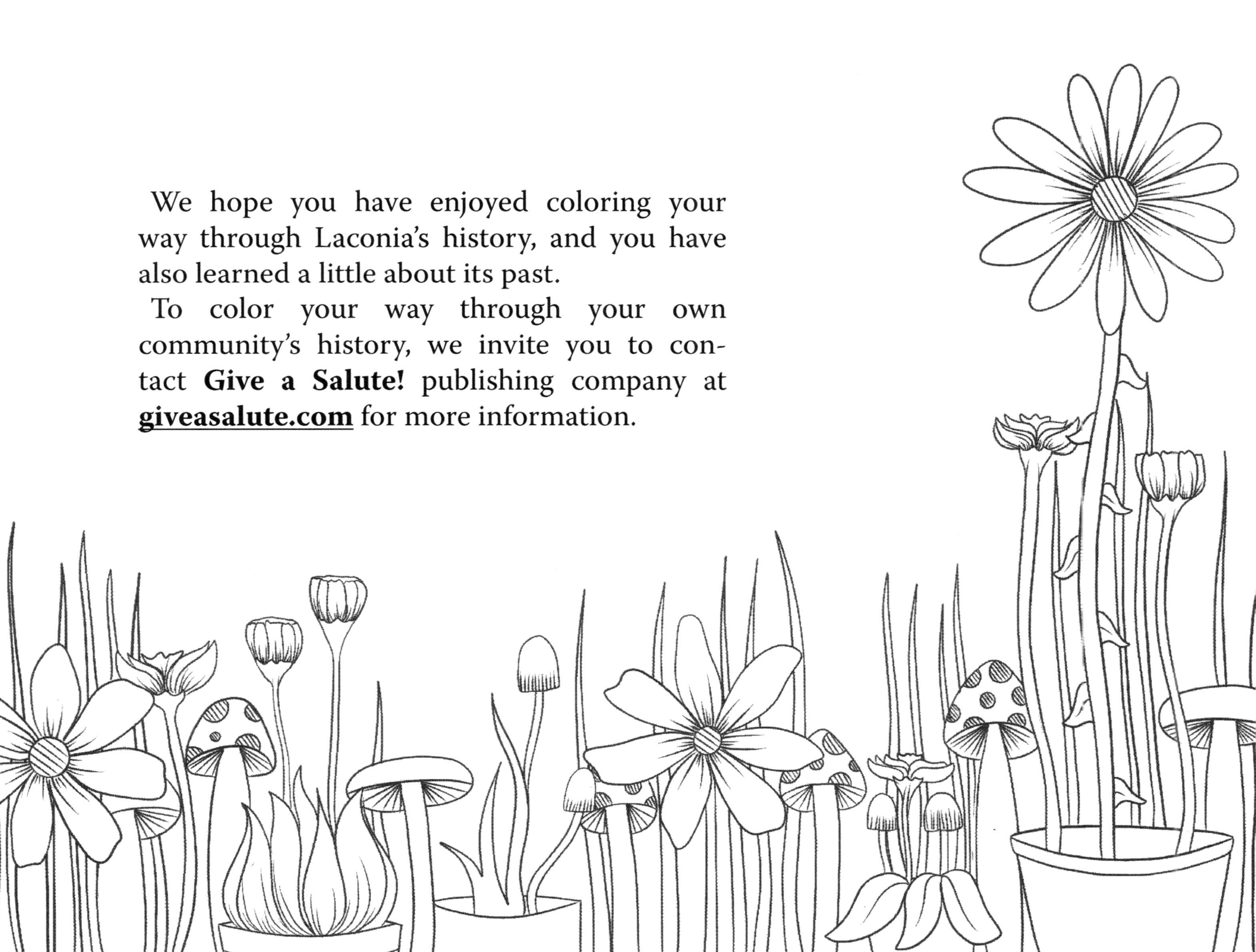

We hope you have enjoyed coloring your way through Laconia's history, and you have also learned a little about its past.

To color your way through your own community's history, we invite you to contact **Give a Salute!** publishing company at **giveasalute.com** for more information.